Monumental Tales
From the Ozarks

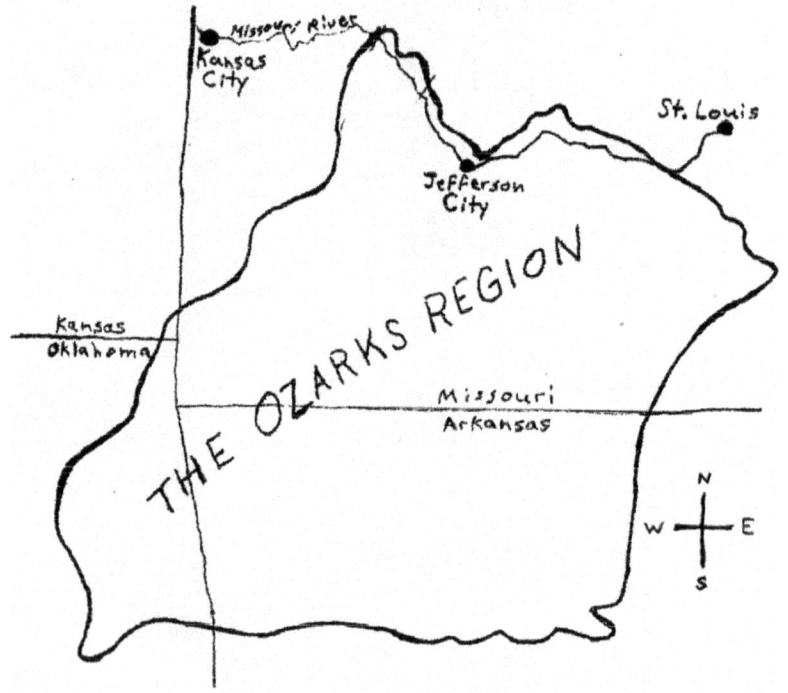

Illustration of the Ozarks region.

Monumental Tales from the Ozarks

Rex T. Jackson

HERITAGE BOOKS
2015

HERITAGE BOOKS
AN IMPRINT OF HERITAGE BOOKS, INC.

Books, CDs, and more—Worldwide

For our listing of thousands of titles see our website at
www.HeritageBooks.com

Published 2015 by
HERITAGE BOOKS, INC.
Publishing Division
5810 Ruatan Street
Berwyn Heights, Md. 20740

Copyright © 2015 Rex T. Jackson

Heritage Books by the author:
A Trail of Tears: The American Indian in the Civil War
James B. Eads: The Civil War Ironclads and His Mississippi
The Sultana Saga: The Titanic of the Mississippi
Monumental Tales from the Ozarks
Traces of Ozarks Past: Outlaws, Icons, and Memorable Events

All rights reserved. No part of this book may be reproduced or transmitted in any form or by any means, electronic or mechanical, including photocopying, recording or by any information storage and retrieval system without written permission from the author, except for the inclusion of brief quotations in a review.

International Standard Book Numbers
Paperbound: 978-0-7884-5631-2
Clothbound: 978-0-7884-6140-8

Monumental Tales From the Ozarks

Contents

1...Nathaniel Lyon: The First Civil War General to Fall
11...Carry A. Nation: The Sunday-Smashing, Hatchet-Swinging Crusader for Prohibition
19...Hornet Spook Light: Unexplained Legend of the Ozarks
23...Monument to Mickey Mantle: A Major League Legend
29...General Franz Sigel's Breakfast and the Skirmish at Bentonville
33...1938 Jesse James Movie Filmed in the Ozarks
41...Deadly Work at the Mount Zion Church
47...Mountain Meadows Massacre: Wagon Train to Disaster
55...The "Boonville Races"
61...Major Jacob Wolf House: Arkansas' Oldest Public Building
67...Destruction of Osceola and the Sauk River Camp
73...Shades of Fort Smith
81...Mills, Resorts, and Spas
89...Road to the Baxter Springs Massacre
97...Memorable Disasters
105...Harvey and Bernice Jones' Har-Ber Village
109...Ha Ha Tonka: R.M. Snyder's Dream Castle Ruins
113...Andrew Carnegie: Libraries of Generosity
119...George Dimmitt Memorial Hospital
123...Old Spanish Fort: Legend and Lore
126...Moses and Stephen Austin: Icons of Missouri and Texas
149...Alf Bolin: The Death of an Ozarks Outlaw

Preface

Monuments that dot the world's landscape remind us from generation to generation of those who came before us; they also mark unforgettable historical events which have taken place. Written in stone are many names and useful signage that can educate, inspire, or move us to tears or action. The Ozarks region of America is no exception, there are many tombstones and numerous monuments scattered throughout its hills and hollows. In some instances, buildings, towns, and various locations can serve as a reminder of the past, like a battleground, courthouse, geological formation, museum, ruins, or some other thing—and, the benefits they offer can deliver the same stimulating rewards.

The Ozarks region of Missouri, Arkansas, Oklahoma, and Kansas has, over the years, been a place where many have migrated or visited. Its state parks, lakes, and attractions have lured a great many of them to come and enjoy. One of the best sources of information and promotion about its culture, businesses, and opportunity, was courtesy of *The Ozarks Mountaineer*, first published in 1952 by Roscoe and Velma Steward. In September 1965, Clay M. Anderson joined the staff and two years later became its owner and editor; he died on October 2, 1993, which left Barbara Wehrman the honor of continuing to publish the popular Branson, Missouri area, Ozarks periodical. Eventually, the magazine was sold and printed its last issue in 2012. Wehrman once said that nobody loved the Ozarks more than Clay Anderson. Left behind are the many printed issues and contributions of its supporters—advertisers, writers, and employees.

Such champions have endeavored to make the Ozarks a successful gathering place, playground, and bustling attraction for residents and tourists alike. The unique history of the region is found in its multitude of monuments, and also in its documentation—magazines like *The Ozarks Mountaineer*, *The Ozarks Reader* (2004-2012), and others; as well as the many books and newspapers that have been published. All of these things serve as reminders of those souls that went before us—showing where we came from and where we may be heading in the future. Surely, anyone interested in American and Ozarks history and concerned about the well-being of the area, should embrace these things.

In the pages of this small volume you can find a sampling of the people, places, and events that have spotlighted the Ozarks region of America. Its ongoing culture and heritage will, hopefully, be one we can look back on with no regret. The Ozarks can be a place where we can live, visit, and enjoy throughout the ages. RTJ

MONUMENTAL TALES FROM THE OZARKS

Monument at the Wilson's Creek National Battlefield near Springfield, Missouri, where Union General Nathaniel Lyon fell.

Nathaniel Lyon: The First Civil War General to Fall

Stories and tales abound concerning America's Civil War. From 1861 to 1865 the nation was in turmoil as the conflict generated no shortage of memorable and monumental events—both big and small. During those bloody years the death-toll soared to about 633,000 souls; and among them were a significant number of well-known officers who gave the last full measure of devotion. Many of them are remembered for various reasons, some for their character, battleground bravery, military tactics, cowardice, foolhardiness and a host of other things that history has attributed to them—but, for Brigadier General Nathaniel Lyon it is, for the most part, the distinction of being the first general to fall in battle as a result of this homegrown war.

Nathaniel Lyon was born in Ashford, Connecticut on July 14, 1818. He attended West Point Military Academy and graduated in 1841, serving in Florida from 1841 to 1842 and in the Mexican War that was waged from 1846 to 1848, where he became a brevetted captain for his work at Churubusco and Contrevas; and he gained further notoriety while serving in frontier warfare in California from 1849 to 1853. After this, he was stationed in Kansas and was a Free Soil advocate until he was sent to St. Louis, Missouri in January 1861, just prior to the outbreak of the Civil War.

Missouri's journey into the war began to brew over the

differences that existed beforehand during the Border War with neighboring Kansas. Likewise, the Dred Scott case at St. Louis and the Missouri Supreme Court decision about the matter further stirred the pot of national agitation.

The election of Abraham Lincoln in November 1860 did little to alleviate the boiling point. The secession of the Southern states, South Carolina, Mississippi, Florida, Alabama, Georgia, Louisiana, and Texas, which happened even before Lincoln's inauguration, quickly followed the election. The act was unacceptable to President Lincoln, who cried: "The Union of these states is perpetual." Lincoln believed that if runaway slaves to the North were not promptly returned, war would have inevitably occurred anyway.

When the new Chief Executive refused to abandon Fort Sumter in Charleston Harbor, South Carolina, its Union garrison was bombarded for thirty-four hours until they surrendered. The day after the surrender of the fort, President Lincoln requested 75,000 troops to "maintain the honor, the integrity, and the existence of the national Union." The South heard his intent loud and clear and four more states seceded form the Union—Arkansas, Virginia, Tennessee, and North Carolina. Southerners believed that they had as much a right to secession as the early American colonists had to sever ties with Great Britain. As a result, Southern President Jefferson Davis called up 100,000 troops of his own to defend the Confederacy from a Northern invasion.

Back in Missouri, a warning was issued to the federal government not to launch an attack of any state. "A State Convention was called; bills to organize, arm, and equip the militia were introduced...." And it was reported that "the people of Missouri would instantly rally on the side of such State to resist the invaders at all hazards and to the last extremity."

Union-loyal Captain Nathaniel Lyon, as a result of these developments, turned his undivided attention to the protection of the St. Louis Arsenal and the capture of Camp Jackson, now established. In an attempt to preserve the Union and resolve growing anti-government sentiment beginning to boil over in the region, Capt. Lyon held a meeting with pro-Southern Missouri Governor Claiborne Fox Jackson and ex-Missouri Governor Major

Nathaniel Lyon

General Sterling Price, and reportedly made his Federal intentions very clear to them, saying: "...rather than concede to the State of Missouri the right to demand that my Government shall not enlist troops within her limits, or bring troops into the State whenever it pleases, or move its own troops at its own will into, out of, or through the State; rather than concede to the State of Missouri for one instant the right to dictate to my Government in any matter, however unimportant, I would see you, and you, and you, and you, and you, and every man, woman, and child in the State, dead and buried."

At a place called Lindell's Grove in St. Louis, Brigadier General Daniel M. Frost under the direction of Governor Jackson had set up Camp Jackson to drill and discipline his 635 militiamen, preparing to seize the St. Louis Arsenal which contained about "60,000 stand of arms and a great abundance of other munitions of war" belonging to the United States government. On the other hand, Capt. Lyon was making plans of his own to capture Jackson's camp with his 7,000 men. When Capt. Lyon learned of a riverboat steamer, *J.C. Swan*, which arrived in St. Louis from Baton Rouge, Louisiana, delivering "a large supply of military stores, including...muskets, ammunition, and cannon" on the night of May 8, 1861, headed for Camp Jackson and the state militia, he became alarmed and even more determined to put an end to Jackson's anti-government encampment and training facility which was obviously being supported by the secessionist South.

In the *Official Records of the Union and Confederate Armies* Lyon reports of his attack on Camp Jackson to Colonel L. Thomas, Adjutant-General U.S. Army, saying that: "Their extraordinary and unscrupulous conduct, and their evident design, and the governor of the State, to take a position of hostility to the United States, are matters of extensive detail and abounding evidence. Having appealed to the South for assistance, every appearance indicated a rapid accumulation of men and means for seizing Government property and overturning its authority. I accordingly foresaw that under the extraordinary measures of the governor and legislature of this State aggressions would soon commence against the General Government on the part of these opposers of it, and of all who in such a state of hostilities, willing to support the State against the Government. Of this there can be no doubt, as also that the issue would be taken by the State as soon as she felt able to sustain it. It was therefore necessary to meet this embarrassing complication as early as possible, and accordingly I proceeded yesterday with a large body of troops, supported by artillery, to the camp...which is situated in the western part of the city...."

After the action taken by Lyon, General Frost complained to Capt. Lyon that the attack was "illegal and unconstitutional." In a letter to General Williams S. Harney, U.S.A., Commanding the Department of the West, Frost writes about his surrender of the camp: "My command was...deprived of their arms, and surrendered into the hands of Captain Lyon. After which, whilst thus disarmed and surrounded, a fire was opened upon a portion of it by his troops, and a number of my men put to death, together with several innocent lookers on—men, women, and children."

Concerning this incident, Capt. Lyon reported that a mob had attacked his force which prompted the death of Frost's men and the other civilian citizens. In *Battles and Leaders of the Civil War* Colonel Thomas L. Snead had this to add: "While the surrender was taking place a great crowd of people, among whom were U.S. Grant and W.T. Sherman, hurried to the scene. Most of the crowd sympathized with the prisoners, and some gave expression to their indignation. One of Lyon's German regiments thereupon opened fire upon them, and twenty-eight men, women, and children were killed."

On May 11, 1861, the day after the surrender of Camp Jackson, Lyon wrote that he marched his prisoners—50 officers and 639 men to the arsenal, but released the majority of them (with the exception of one captain that declined his parole) the next day.

The anti-Union sentiment only increased as a result of the killing of the innocent citizens. Before long, the streets of Jefferson City filled up with angry Missourians ready and willing to take up arms and volunteer in the state's defense, and Major General Sterling Price was on hand to deliver a "moving" speech that prompted his listeners to offer their service to the Southern cause.

About Gen. Price, General Dabnery H. Maury later wrote:

Nathaniel Lyon

"General Price was one of the handsomest men I have every seen...A braver or kinder heart beat in no man's bosom; he was wise in counsel, bold in action, and never spared his own blood in any battlefield. No man had greater influence over his troops...it was impossible to find a more magnificent specimen of manhood in his prime than Sterling Price presented to the brave Missourians, who loved him with a fervor not less than we Virginians felt for [Robert E.] Lee."

After the affair at Camp Jackson, Lyon proceeded to disperse the state's pro-Southern forces of Jackson and Price from the Missouri River town of Boonville, who was forced to make a hasty retreat—some referred to the rout as the "Boonville Races." As a result, Price decided to head for southwest Missouri to get closer to the safety of Confederate Arkansas. Lyon had about 2,350 men at his command and Jackson and Price had about 6,000 men and seven artillery pieces. However, it was Union Colonel Franz Sigel who confronted their southern retreat just north of Carthage with only 1,100 men and eight big guns, "hoping to either defeat him or hold him in check till Lyon could arrive and destroy him."

The *first* significant land battle of the American Civil War did not go well for the Union—Col. Sigel was outnumbered and Price's superior army soon forced the Federals to abandon the struggle. Afterwards, the Missouri secessionists headed even deeper into the Ozarks to Cowskin Prairie (McDonald County) and began their training for the many historic battles that would follow.

In *The First Year of the War in Missouri* found in *Battles and Leaders of the Civil War*, Colonel Thomas L. Snead had this to report about the training-time at Cowskin Prairie: "...Price had us all ready for the field in less than three weeks. We had no tents, it is true, but tents would have been in our way; we had no uniforms, but a bit of flannel or calico fastened to the shoulder of an officer designated his rank sufficiently for all practical proposes; the ripening corn-fields were our depots of subsistence; the prairies furnished forage, and the people in defense of whose homes we were eager to fight gladly gave us of all their stores."

The upcoming and inevitable bloody engagement at Wilson's Creek left Federal troops moving from Springfield and Confederate forces marching from Barry County and Cassville. In Goodspeed's *History of Barry County* it reports that "On July 25, 1861, Gen. Price moved from Elk River [Cowskin Prairie] in McDonald County to Cassville, where he was joined by McCulloch and Pearce on the 29th. Gen. Price at this time joined Pearce's division, while Greer's Texas Rangers, and Gen. Rains' battalion of mounted Missourians, joined forces on August 1 and 2. It was with the intention of attacking this large force at Cassville that Gen. Lyon set out on that march which resulted in the disastrous affair at Wilson's Creek in August, 1861."

The first skirmish of the two armies occurred at a place called Dug Springs, when Price's advance guard engaged Lyon's Federal troops who were on the Cassville Road (also known as the Fayetteville Road) on August 2, 1861. In *Battles and Leaders of the Civil War* it showcases Lyon's leadership and determination: "During those blistering August days the men marched with bleeding feet and parched lips, Lyon himself urging forward the weary and footsore stragglers."

After the action at Dug Springs, Gen. Lyon fell back to Springfield to regroup and to beg Major General John C. Fremont, Commanding the Western Department at St. Louis, for much needed reinforcements. In a final letter to Fremont after hearing that there would be no aid coming, a brave Lyon replied: "...I find my position extremely embarrassing, and am at present unable to determine whether I shall be able to maintain my ground or forced to retire. I shall hold my ground as long as possible, though I may, without knowing how far, endanger the safety of my entire force...."

As for the Confederates, Price was eager to advance but General Ben McCulloch wanted to retreat. In the end, Lyon received no help from Fremont and the Confederate authorities ordered an advance.

A plan of action was devised by Gen. Lyon, Gen. T.W. Sweeney, Col. Franz Sigel, and Maj. S.D. Sturgis to make a surprise attack on the Confederates who occupied nearby Wilson's Creek. And McCulloch, who now wanted "command of the consolidated army," heard from Price: "I am not fighting for distinction, but for the liberties of my country, and I am willing to surrender not only my command but my life, if necessary, as a sacrifice to the cause."

At the Battle of Wilson's Creek on August 10, 1861, Lyon moved on the Southern forces of McCulloch and Price at daybreak. Lyon "went at the head of the column," according to *Battles and Leaders of the Civil War*, "and when the action opened he kept his place at the front, entering the heat of the engagement with the line, near Totten's battery. He maintained an imperturbable coolness, and his eyes shone with the ardor of conflict. He directed, encouraged, and rallied his troops in person, sending his staff in all directions, and was frequently without an attendant except one or two faithful orderlies."

Before long, however, Lyon's horse was killed and he was wounded in his leg and head and he became "begrimed and bloody." As the battle-smoke thickened upon the field the "carnage became frightful. The slopes of Bloody Hill were strewn with ghastly corpses...Lyon fought like a demon...Price charged time and again up the slope, only to be repulsed by the Federals lying on the crest."

Lyon was eventually given another horse and he again somehow managed to ride to the front "Swinging his hat and calling to his men to follow." It was at this time that Lyon was shot in the left side of his breast and was prompted to dismount his horse. He was helped to the ground by Private Ed. Lehman, and with his last dying breath reportedly said: "Lehman, I am killed." The historic place where the first general of the American Civil War fell was dubbed: "Bloody Point."

After the death of Lyon, Maj. Sturgis assumed command. The Battle of Wilson's Creek raged on until after 11 o'clock when the Union forces retreated back to Springfield, reaching there about 5 o'clock that evening—the battle had lasted about six hours.

Gen. McCulloch recalled some of the horrors of the action in his official report: "The incessant roll of musketry was deafening, and the balls fell thick as hailstones, but still our gallant Southerners pushed onward, and with one wild yell broke upon the enemy, pushing them back and strewing the ground with their dead."

The body of Nathaniel Lyon was first taken by wagon to the Ray House which was being used as a field hospital and examined by Dr. Melcher. Lyon's remains were treated as well as the circumstances could permit and were taken to Springfield to the house of John S. Phelps—Lyon's former headquarters. Since only Mary W. Phelps was at home, she assumed charge of the general's body and had it placed, temporarily, in a fruit cellar for safekeeping until it was buried in her garden. However, his body was eventually removed from the "shallow" grave and transported to its permanent resting place in his home state of Connecticut and buried with full military honors.

The American Civil War harvested the lives of many of its participants, including officers and generals, like Thomas J. ("Stonewall") Jackson, James E.B. ("Jeb") Stuart, James B. McPherson, and Ben McCulloch to name a few; even the Chief Executive, Abraham Lincoln, eventually paid the ultimate price. The stories and legends of that era will, no doubt, continue to be spun for future generations. But, the monumental distinction of being the first casualty of high rank will forever belong to Brigadier General Nathaniel Lyon who fell in the Ozarks.

Bibliography

Battles and Leaders of the Civil War, The Century Company, 1887.

Goodspeed's *History of Barry County*, Goodspeed Publishing Company, 1888.

Holcombe and Adams, *An Account of the Battle of Wilson's Creek, or Oak Hills*, Dow and Adams, Publishers, Springfield, Missouri, 1883.

Official Records of the Union and Confederate Armies, Washington: Government Printing Office, 1881.

Webb, W.L., *Battles and Biographies of Missourians* or the *Civil War Period of Our State*, Hudson-Kimberly Publishing Company, Kansas City, Missouri, 1900.

Reproduction Old West saloon at Harbor Village in Grove, Oklahoma.

Carry A. Nation: The Sunday-Smashing, Hatchet-Swinging Crusader for Prohibition

American citizens who enjoyed alcoholic beverages, like a glass of wine or a beer at mealtime, were out-of-luck between 1919 and 1933—thanks to the Eighteenth Amendment that prohibited the manufacture, sale, or use of alcohol. When Congress enacted the Jones Law in 1929, such persons convicted of making liquor, importing, exporting, selling, and transporting it could be imprisoned for five long years and fined as much as $10,000.

This nationwide adoption of this so-called "noble experiment" resulted in the decrease of its consumption, especially in rural areas, but it also gave rise to widespread lawlessness. Makeshift stills produced "moonshine" and city-dwellers made "bathtub gin." Speakeasies sprang up to cater to the multitudes as illicit liquor was supplied by bootleggers (named for the bottles they hid in their tall boots), as well as many smugglers and rumrunners who brought it into the United States from places like Canada, Cuba, and Mexico.

By 1925, however, a lot of opposition to the law was gaining momentum, and by 1927 the Association Against the Prohibition Amendment was established. The liquor raids and seizures by law enforcement agents finally ended when the Eighteenth Amendment was repealed by ratification of the Twenty-first Amendment in 1933.

Social issues are oftentimes drawn-out into the forefront and, debate, controversy, division, and even violence becomes commonplace. During this early part of the 1900s, tobacco, spirits, and equal voting rights for all citizens were hot topics in America. In hindsight, concerning these issues, we can now better appreciate the directional logic that was adopted by the majority—historical studies we can now benefit from. During that difficult time in our nation's past however, one name that rises to the surface of the quagmire is Carrie Nation, who fought for Prohibition using some rather controversial techniques that catapulted her to national notoriety. Her infamous work cleared a path to the ongoing stories still being told of her colorful life and times.

Carrie Amelia Moore was born in Garrard County in rural Kentucky on November 25, 1846, to George and Mary Moore. George was a plantation and slave owner and Mary, who gave birth to six children, was said to have suffered from mental illness and, reportedly, thought that she was the queen of England. Young Carrie spent much of her time with the slaves and grew up in their close company—which, as some believe, may have had something to do with her mother's state-of-mind. Overtime, Carrie was educated in various places in Kentucky, Missouri, and Texas—by the outbreak of the American Civil War the Moore family had settled in the Lone Star state.

On November 21, 1867, twenty-one-year-old Carrie married Dr. Charles Gloyd, a physician. She gave birth to a daughter, Charlien, who exhibited signs of emotional problems. Carrie became a teacher but before long the marriage was in trouble, mostly attributed to her husband's increasing abuse of alcohol. Eventually, Carrie left him and he died not long afterwards.

In 1877, Carrie wed Dr. David A. Nation, a newspaper editor, attorney, and Christian minister. They moved to Medicine Lodge, Kansas in 1889, where the use of liquor had been outlawed; here, Carrie hoped her second husband would not partake of the substance—he did. While in Medicine Lodge, Carrie founded a branch of the Woman's Christian Temperance Union and claimed to have received a divine calling to attack any establishment that sold alcohol; including pharmacies that stocked it for medicinal purposes.

Carry A. Nation

Carrie argued about religion with her preacher husband and even helped to write his Sunday sermons by including judgmental remarks about users of tobacco and alcohol. She contended that she had been graced with special instructions directly from God and from the fire of the Holy Spirit. By and by she changed the spelling of her name to Carry—hence, her "movement could help carry a nation." She believed that the name would be more marketable. For several years Carry gave spirited speeches and also held public prayer meetings, disregarding and contradicting the teachings of Jesus Christ who taught, according to Matthew 6:6: "But thou, when thou prayest, enter into thy closet, and when thou hast shut thy door, pray to thy Father, which is in secret; and thy Father, which seeth in secret, shall reward thee openly." Carry's message targeted and condemned such things as the evils of consuming alcohol, fraternal orders, smoking, short skirts, and many, many other things. Carry went so far as to applaud the death and assassination of United States President William McKinley, because she judged him to be a drinking man. And once again she found herself divorced in 1901 because she chose not to have a physical, loving relationship with her husband, which resulted in a childless second marriage.

As time passed she gained a number of followers for her self-appointed cause and along with rocks, bricks, Bible, and her signature hatchet began to make a name for herself in the annals of American history. In the Carey Hotel barroom in Wichita, Kansas on December 27, 1900, Carry A. Nation began her "smashing crusade" when she, according to a local newspaper, "...boldly marched into the bar room at the hotel followed by several of the disciples and going behind the bar, drove the barkeeper from his post and deliberately broke the...mirror. She then crossed the room and threw a stone through a magnificent oil painting. The police interfered at this point and the women were hustled out of the place."

The painting which she demolished that day at the Carey Hotel was the *Cleopatra At Her Bath*, a work of art she decided was too risqué and filthy. On the other hand, her religious-driven work began to attract national attention, as Nation continued her "hatchetation" rampage in other places. On one occasion, Nation was said to have been arrested by county officers on three warrants "as she came out of the First Christian church." Nation would say such things as: "It has been left to a handful of women, with their little hatchets...to do the work of the Lord." Between 1900 and 1910 she was arrested thirty times for her saloon crimes and disturbing the peace. The proceeds that she made from her speeches, and the sale of her souvenir hatchets which she sold, paid for her bail and fines during this time.

One of Nation's statements, in part, went like this: "We have proven that the commands of Jesus is the only safe way. 'Resist the devil and he will flee.' Non-resist and he is bold and defiant.

"This army of the Home Defenders declares its intent in his name. We are the fathers and mothers who, God's host, have come to the help of the Lord against the mighty and we are here to withstand all the 'fiery darts of the wicked' with the shield of faith. We demand defense and we will have it. No whisky, no tobacco or profanity shall defile our hearthstones. No man or woman who uses any of these defilements shall have or need ask to serve us. We will be your brother to help you to cleanse yourself from the filthiness of the flesh...We are going to place before the people men and women who must be examples of virtue and strength, who shall serve us to reward good and punish evil...Kansas shall be free and we will set her on a hill that her light may go to every dark corner of the earth...."

Nation's vigilante-point was made by chopping up whiskey barrels, smashing to smithereens bar fixtures, busting bottles and glasses, mirrors, windows, doors, kegs of beer, and many other things during her hatchet-wielding mission of spreading her interpretation of righteousness; as well as spewing judgmental tirades in the process. Her radical sexist opinion of men was that they were "nicotine-soaked, beer-besmirched, whiskey-greased, red-eyed devils."

Nation became well-known and eventually published a newsletter called *The Smashers Mail*, and a newspaper she dubbed, appropriately, *The Hatchet*. She appeared in vaudeville shows, wrote an autobiography titled *The Use and Need of the Life of Carry Nation* published in 1904, and disliked the major political parties in

Carry A. Nation

favor of the Prohibition Party.
At the end of her life she moved to Eureka Springs, Arkansas, where her home became a boarding house and school, which she called the National College. Ironically, however, Nation found herself "strapped for cash" and her daughter, Charlien, who had been committed in 1905 to the Texas State Asylum, had recovered to some degree and had married a man that owned a number of saloons in Texas, and occasionally sent money for her mother's needs.

On January 13, 1911, while delivering one of her speeches in Eureka Springs, Carry collapsed from a heart attack and fell into a coma. She was taken to the Evergreen Place Hospital in Leavenworth, Kansas, and eventually died on June 9, 1911. Dual services were held in Eureka Springs and at Kansas City, Kansas. The Kansas City *Star*, June 10, 1911, carried the details: "Funeral services for Mrs. Carry A. Nation, who died last night in Leavenworth, will be in Kansas City, Kas. Mrs. M.D. Moore, the sister-in-law of Mrs. Nation, was with her when she died, and the services will be at 10 o'clock tomorrow morning at the home of Mrs. Moore, 704 Reynolds Avenue. The Rev. W.S. Lowe, pastor of the Central Christian Church, Kansas City, Kas., will conduct the services. The burial will be in Belton, Mo., where Mrs. Nation's parents are buried."

Carry A. Nation was buried at the Belton City Cemetery in Belton, Missouri; she was 65-years-old at the time of her death. The Eighteenth Amendment, which banned intoxicating liquors, was ratified in 1919—only eight years after her death. It was the beginning of America's failed Prohibition experiment. In 1924, because her gravesite was unmarked, the Woman's Christian Temperance Union erected a stone, which read: "Faithful to the cause of Prohibition, she hath done what she could."

The house that Nation had lived in at Medicine Lodge, Kan., became a National Historic Landmark in the 1950s; Nation's boarding house in Eureka Springs, Ark., became a museum called Hatchet Hall. The "Sunday Smasher" who led an army of fanatical disciples attempting to spread their gospel and make converts by force, and who was also known to snatch pipes and cigars out of the mouths of grown men, left a legacy that continues to carry a nation to the wisdom buried in its past.

Bibliography

The Barber County *Index*, January 15, 1902.

The American Promise: A History of the United States, Bedford Books, Boston, 1998.

Enss, Chris, *Tales Behind the Tombstones*, The Globe Pequot Press, Guilford, Connecticut, 2007.

Funk & Wagnalls New Encyclopedia, Funk & Wagnalls, Inc., New York, 1979.

Jackson, Rex T., *Carrie A. Nation: The Bible-Totting, Hatchet Wielding, Advocate of Prohibition*, Vol. 9, No. 2, 2012, The Ozarks Reader Magazine, Neosho, Missouri.

Kansas City *Star*, February 18, 1901; and June 10, 1911.

Hornet Cemetery located in Hornet, Missouri.

Hornet Spook Light: Unexplained Legend of the Ozarks

Wild ghost stories and tall tales of haunting and the unexplained have been a part of life since earliest times. Spooks and apparitions of fog-like sightings of the dead have been reported time and again—especially at night when wolves and coyotes howl, the wind blows and rustles the leaves, and owls hoot. These restless souls may hover and linger among us here on earth because they may have unfinished business or, perhaps, they have not received a proper burial complete with genuine mourners. For whatever the reason, the embodiment of these nonmaterial beings continues to be a source of wonder in movies, folklore, legend, and storytelling.

On many occasions Ozarkians have reported seeing strange lights in the dark of night—when they can be seen. These ghostly figures have been hard to prove and continue to elude reasonable explanation. They have been observed in swampy areas, graveyards, marshlands, haunted houses, boggy grounds and in remote places. Native Americans regarded orbs of unexplained lights as "fire creatures" or as an omen of death; they sometimes believed them to be wandering souls. The phenomenon has been known worldwide by many things, such as "spook lights", "ghost lights", "foxfire", "will-o-the-wisp", "graveyard lights", "churchyard lights", "Indian lights", "ball lightning", "corpse candle", "jack-o-lantern", "friar's lantern", "hobby lantern" and many other colorful things. In Latin the lights are known as *ignus fatuus*, which means "foolish fire."

One common place where mysterious sightings have been known to appear is in graveyards. Some contend that the spontaneous combustion of methane, which can be produced by decaying matter, is the cause of the fiery lights known as will-o-the-wisp and all the other names associated with burial ground sightings. Still others believe that the weird lights might be created by phosphorus (found in corpses) seeping out from the gravesites.

Some eerie manifestations have been spied in the Ozark timberlands. The foxfire is thought to emanate from rotting logs, limbs, and other wooded matter found in the forests. The phosphorescent light is caused by a type of glow-in-the-dark luminous fungus (*Armillaria mellea*) produced as a result of the decaying process. However, this explanation is little comfort to the frightened, unsuspecting victims of the foxfire while wandering about the woods after dark.

One stubborn, well-known paranormal legend in the Ozarks region is the Hornet Spook Light, often seen between the small hamlet of Hornet, Missouri and Quapaw, Oklahoma; just south of Joplin, Mo. Most of the sightings occur on a stretch of road dubbed the "Devil's Promenade." Also known as the "Tri-State Spook Light" and the "Ozark Spook Light," the strange lights have been reported to vary in size from a tennis ball to as big as a washtub. Whenever approached or chased, however, the orbs of light retreat or suddenly disappear. Many who have tried to discredit the occurrence have put forth the notion that the spooky lights are caused by swamp gas, car headlights, pranks, ball lightning and other things. One explanation for the lights has been electrical atmospheric charges generated by tectonic strain. It is believed that a faultline runs from the Quapaw-Hornet area to New Madrid, Missouri where a massive earthquake occurred in 1811 and the shifting and movement deep below the ground is responsible for the electrical discharges of light. The car headlights have been ruled out, for the most part, because Native Americans and early pioneers reported seeing the lights there long before the invention of the horseless carriage.

Over the years, ghost stories have been handed down to explain

Hornet Spook Light

the Hornet Spook Light: One tale is told of an Osage Indian chief who was beheaded by his angry wife during a dispute, and that the apparition is merely the spirit of the headless chieftain searching for his severed head; while another story contends that a Quapaw Indian maiden supposedly drowned herself in a nearby river after she had received the heartbreaking news that her brave-warrior-lover had fallen in battle. The light is her restless spirit haunting the places they once knew in their earthly lives; and still another legend tells of a miner who returned home to find that hostile Indians had attacked his cabin in his absence and his family had been abducted. The unexplained light is the ghost of the miner still frantically hunting for his missing wife and children.

Investigations have been mounted on several occasions to discover the secrets of the Hornet Spook Light, by the Army Corps of Engineers, various paranormal and scientific groups, amateur ghost hunters and sleuths, and even by the once popular television show "Unsolved Mysteries." As a result of their studies, the truth concerning the strange lights remains a mystery to this day.

The unexplained can be nothing more than a hoax, or maybe it can, like the Hornet Spook Light, stubbornly continue to stump its audience. When under the cover and gloom of darkness near a cemetery, woodlands, or the Devil's Promenade Road on the Oklahoma-Missouri border and you see a mysterious light, it might be a flashlight, car headlight, or some other worldly thing—but, it could be something else that defies ordinary reason or explanation, maybe something nonmaterial that can light up the night and send a bone-chilling charge up and down your flesh and spine.

Bibliography

Funk & Wagnalls New Encyclopedia, Funk & Wagnalls, Inc., New York, 1979.

Jackson, Rex T., *Mysterious Lights Haunt the Ozarks*, Vol. 8, No. 1, 2011, The Ozarks Reader Magazine, Neosho, Missouri.

Mahnkey, Douglas, *Hill and Holler Stories*, S of O Press, School of the Ozarks, 1975.

Merriam Webster's Dictionary, Merriam-Webster, Inc., 1996.

Monument to Mickey Mantle in Commerce, Oklahoma.

Monument to Mickey Mantle: A Major League Legend

Many Americans and fans from all-over-the-world share in common a love affair with the game of baseball. The professional athletes with colorful names and uniforms, the bright lights, the "crack" of the wooden bat, "pop" of the glove, the called "strike three," or the unforgettable homerun brings a deafening, earsplitting roar from the stadium grandstand. They gather in multitudes to see their favorite team or player perform—and, perhaps, break new records, win the pennant, the World Series or an induction into the state or national sports Hall of Fame. These exciting great moments in baseball, America's favorite pastime, has not been overlooked in the Ozarks.

There have been a number of books created about America's sport, such as the tragic fictional tale of the "mighty" Casey who endured a game-losing strikeout as a member of the Mudville Nine. Mark Twain wrote about the game and said that it was: "…the very symbol, the outward and visible expression, of the drive and push and struggle of the raging, tearing, booming nineteenth century."

Primitive versions of baseball were played as early as the end of the eighteenth century; one variation was played in New York City, New York and was called "one old cat." By 1835, there were games being played called "town ball" and "New York ball." The foundation of modern baseball, however, began in 1845 with the establishment of the Knickerbockers Baseball Club, which played their debut game on June 19, 1846, at Hoboken, New Jersey—they lost to a group of amateur players called the New York Nine by an overwhelming score of 23 to 1. The Knickerbockers were, for the most part, a bunch of volunteer firemen from Manhattan. The rout was due in large part to the fact that a number of the best players for the Knickerbockers decided not to cross the Hudson River to play at the Elysian Field in Hoboken.

By the mid-1860s, baseball had become evermore popular in America and by 1869 the Cincinnati Red Stockings introduced it as a professional sport. In 1871, the National Association of Professional Baseball Players was created; the National League of Professional Baseball Clubs came in 1876; and the American League followed in 1900. The World Series was inaugurated as a postseason two-league playoff series three years later on October 13, 1903. The Pittsburgh Nationals faced-off against the Boston Americans who took the series five games to three in America's first World Series. The final game was played at Boston's Huntington Avenue Ball Field. Spectators enjoyed seeing players like Cy Young, Honus Wagner, and Patrick Henry Dougherty. The Baseball Hall of Fame and Museum opened in Cooperstown, New York in 1939; and since then many players have been inducted.

To attract even more fans, the sale of beer and cheap seats drew larger crowds; and playing games on Sunday became a popular tradition—much to the objections of the Protestants. The "color barrier" was finally smashed in 1947 when Jackie Robinson, an African American, joined the Brooklyn Dodgers. Robinson was born in Georgia—his father was a sharecropper and his father before him was a slave. As a result of his acceptance to the major leagues, some Southern-born players threatened not to play; and a couple of baseball clubs even went so far as to talk of striking. Jackie Robinson fought back and played until 1956, enduring racial taunting and being banned from restaurants and hotels because of his skin color. His example paved the way for many others, like Larry Doby who became the first African American in the American League shortly after Robinson was signed. Over-the-years scores of talented athletes have come and gone, but in the Ozarks no name shines brighter than Mickey Mantle.

Mickey Charles Mantle was born in Spavinaw, Oklahoma in

Monument to Mickey Mantle

1931, but relocated to Commerce, Okla. with his family in 1935. Elven "Mutt" Mantle, Mickey's father, was employed in the lead and zinc mines in Commerce. In his "off time" Mutt played semiprofessional baseball; he also dared to dream the dream of a better life for his son than working in the mines. Mantle named his son after Mickey Cochrane, a major league catcher for the Detroit Tigers. Mutt would go on to teach Mickey everything he knew about the sport, and more.

Mickey's father would encourage him to hit from both sides of the plate, which enabled Mickey to bat right-handed and left-handed—this helps a batter hit both right and left-handed pitchers. Mickey pitched and played infield for Commerce High School. He also played football, and this is where he received his first of many injuries. As a result, Mickey learned that he had a rare bone disease called *osteomyelitis*. Regardless of the handicap he continued to play baseball.

A scout for the New York Yankees, by chance, took notice of Mantle at a game in Commerce and offered him the opportunity-of-a-lifetime to play minor league baseball in Independence and Joplin, Missouri. By the spring of 1951, he had joined the New York Yankees as an outfielder.

Mantle's first experience in the "big" leagues didn't go well and by that summer he was back in the minor leagues playing at Kansas City, Mo.—he struggled there as well but not for long. After a visit from his father who gave him a bit of "tough love" advice—a wake up call, Mantle turned it around and was soon back with the Yankees. Mutt would live long enough to see his son play in the 1951 World Series, where the "Yanks" beat the Giants 4 games to 2.

Mantle went on to win the American League's Most Valuable Player award in 1956 with a batting average of .353, 130 runs batted in (RBIs), and 52 homers. In 1961, Mantle and a teammate, Roger Maris, dueled back and forth as homerun "kings"—Mantle hit 54 and Maris ended the season with 61 to break the old standing record held by the famous Babe Ruth. However, a controversy arose over the number of games it took Maris to accomplish the feat. (Babe Ruth hit 60 in a 154-game season while Maris achieved his 61 in a 162-game season.) Mantle won his third MVP award in 1963. He

MONUMENTAL TALES FROM THE OZARKS

was finally moved to first base in 1967 and finished his eventful career as a household name. He died in 1995.

The people of Commerce, Okla. never forgot their hometown hero. On June 12, 2010, a 900-pound statue of the major leaguer was unveiled at the Mickey Mantle Monument Park and Mickey Mantle Field located on historic Route 66. The monument is 9 feet tall and sits on a large base that is 5 feet tall. On one side the base reads "Mickey Charles Mantle," and on the other side is inscribed "A Great Teammate." The $50,000 statue was created by Nick Calcagno, a local artist, and was paid for by the state of Oklahoma. Mickey's son, Danny, was in attendance at the unveiling ceremony.

The sport of baseball continues on and still spawns legends of the game and Hall of Fame stars like Mickey Mantle. They come from many parts of the world where baseball has blossomed and taken root. In the old mining town of Commerce, Okla., an impressive monument to one Ozarkian boy stands firm as a testament to the monumental accomplishments that would make any father proud.

Bibliography

The American Journey: A History of the United States, Prentice Hall, Upper Saddle River, New Jersey, 1998.

Chronicle of America, Chronicle Publications, Inc., Mount Kisco, New York, 1989.

Craft, David, *Great Moments in Baseball*, Metro Books, 1997.

Funk & Wagnalls New Encyclopedia, Funk & Wagnalls, Inc., New York, 1979.

Hollander, Zander, *Great American Athletes of the 20th Century*, Random House, New York, 1966.

Historic marker in downtown Bentonville, Arkansas.

General Franz Sigel's Breakfast and the Skirmish at Bentonville

Near Bentonville, Arkansas, at a local farmstead on March 5, 1862, Union Brigadier General Franz Sigel and his troops were bivouacking waiting for intelligence to the strength, whereabouts, and intentions of the Confederate army. At this time, the Confederates had been very secretive as to their movements when word finally arrived to General Sigel that the enemy was only about a day's march from his encampment at Mckisick's Farm. In the wee hours of the morning of March 6, about 2 o'clock, Gen. Sigel gave the order to move towards the village of Bentonville.

Gen. Sigel had at his command the "Advance guard, under Asboth: One company of Fourth Missouri Cavalry (Fremont Hussars); Second Ohio Battery, under command of Lieutenant Chapman; Fifteenth Missouri Volunteers, under command of Colonel Joliat. Train of First and Second Divisions, escorted and guarded by detachments of the respective regiments. The First Division, under Colonel Osterhaus. The Flying battery, the Fifth Missouri Cavalry (Benton Hussars), and the squadron of the Thirty-sixth Illinois Cavalry, Captain Jenks."

After arriving in Bentonville, Sigel halted to find out whether or not the Southerners were "approaching in strong force, and whether he was advancing from Smith's Mill on the road to Bentonville, or Osage Springs, or on both roads at the same time...." He stayed there with his 600 men and a 6-gun battery taking time that morning to grab a bite-to-eat at the Eagle Hotel, while he waited for word.

Gen. Sigel's breakfast, however, was interrupted by the enemy troop masses of infantry and cavalry moving in from all directions. (Later, after the end of the Civil War, Franz Sigel returned to Bentonville and commented on his disrupted meal, saying that "he had come back to finish" it—a historic marker just off the west side of the town square commemorates the monumental event.)

Colonel Nemett and the Benton Hussars, who had been sent out to reconnoiter and report back, brought the word to Sigel that he had met the "enemy's cavalry, and...several thousand men, cavalry, and infantry were forming in line of battle about a mile from Bentonville on the open fields south of the village."

In response to the arrival of Confederate General Sterling Price's advance guard, Sigel took command and ordered his troops to engage the enemy. In the *Official Records of the Union and Confederate Armies* Gen. Sigel made his report: "...the column moved forward to break through the lines of the enemy, who had already taken position in our front and in both flanks, whilst he appeared behind us in the town in line of battle, re-enforced by some pieces of artillery. The troops advanced slowly, fighting and repelling the enemy in front, flankward, and rear, wherever he stood or attacked.

"From the moment we left the town, at 10:30 in the morning, until 3:30 o'clock in the afternoon, when we met the first re-enforcements—the Second Missouri, the Twenty-fifth Illinois, and a few companies of the Forty-fourth Illinois—we sustained three regular attacks, and were uninterruptedly in sight and under fire of the enemy."

Somehow, Sigel and his men were able to escape and join forces with Union General Samuel R. Curtis at nearby Pea Ridge who was faced off with the Confederation of Earl Van Dorn, Ben McCulloch, Sterling Price, and Albert Pike's Indians—for a two-day battle on March 7-8, 1862, that would leave, when it was all said and done, a total of about 2,000 men killed or wounded on the ghastly battleground at Leetown and Pea Ridge.

About the engagement that day at Bentonville, Sigel reported in the *Official Records* that it "would take too much time to go into detail of this most extraordinary and critical affair, but as a matter of justice I feel it is my duty to declare that according to my humble opinion never troops have shown themselves worthier to defend a great cause than on this day of the 6th of March."

In *Battles and Biographies of Missourians*, W.L. Webb contends that "While the battle of Pea Ridge was a Federal victory, gained principally by Sigel, Van Dorn carried away some of the substantial fruits of success, having captured three hundred prisoners, four pieces of artillery, and three baggage wagons."

And while most Civil War historians agree that the Battle of Pea Ridge was a two-day battle, Annie Heloise Abel who authored *The American Indian as Participant in the Civil War*, wrote: "The Battle of Pea Ridge, in its preliminary stages, was already being fought. It was a three day fight, counting the skirmish at Bentonville on the sixth between General Franz Sigel's detachment and General Sterling Price's advance guard as the work of the first day. The real battle comprised the engagement at Leetown on the seventh and that at Elkhorn Tavern on the eighth."

Whether the Battle of Pea Ridge (or Elkhorn Tavern) could include Sigel's work at Bentonville adding to a three-day battle— will, no doubt, continue to be a source of some debate and speculation. Regardless, the skirmish at Bentonville prompted Major-General Franz Sigel after the war to return there and reminisce about the day when his morning breakfast was so rudely interrupted by America's Civil War.

Bibliography

Abel, Annie Heloise, *The American Indian as Participant in the Civil War*, Arthur H. Clark Company, Cleveland, 1919.

Official Records of the Union and Confederate Armies, Washington: Government Printing Office, 1881.

Sigel, Franz, *Battles and Leaders of the Civil War*, The Century Company, 1887.

Webb, W.L., *Battles and Biographies of Missourians* or *Civil War Period of Our State*, Hudson-Kimberly Publishing Company, Kansas City, Missouri, 1900.

The old McDonald County Courthouse used in the Jesse James movie.

1938 Jesse James Movie Filmed in the Ozarks

When it comes to western outlaws, no name comes to mind more than the notorious Jesse James. His short but eventful life has spawned many opinions, study, and debate concerning him and his infamous work. Some contend that he was and, all of those like him, nothing more than psychopathic thieves and murderers, while others argue that his actions were, for the most part, justly taken or he had no other recourse.

There have been a number of tales spun, books and magazine articles written, and television shows and movies produced—all telling about his daring escapes and adventures. Since a large part of his activities occurred in and around the Ozarks region, it is appropriate that a movie called "Jesse James" was filmed in Pineville, Missouri, in 1938.

The turmoil that led up to the Civil War and, the conflict and period of Reconstruction that followed, created, as some believe, a number of legendary outlaws whose names still linger and reverberate in the annals of American history. Opposing views of their work have oftentimes arisen from the fact and fiction left in the wake of the aftermath. The monumental amount of interest leftover in this lawless era gave Hollywood the incentive and inspiration to undertake yet another attempt at the life and times of Jesse James in motion pictures.

Jesse Woodson James was born on the family farm located near Centerville (Kearney), Missouri, in Clay County, on September 5,

1847, to Robert Sallee and Zerelda Elizabeth James; his brother, Alexander Frank James, also a significant figure in American history was born four years earlier on January 10, 1843. Robert James met Zerelda Cole while attending a religious revival. The two were married at Stamping Ground, Kentucky on December 28, 1841.

Robert and Zerelda James would eventually relocate to Missouri where they would purchase their 275-acre farm. Robert became a Christian minister for the New Hope Baptist Church, while Zerelda gave birth to Frank, Robert (lived only one month), Jesse, and finally Susan Lavenia on November 25, 1849. During this time Reverend James would found two churches and help to establish William Jewell College in nearby Liberty. However, gold fever would entice Robert along with some friends and church members in 1850 to head west to California. Disaster struck the James family shortly after when word came back to them of the sudden death of Robert at the Placerville Gold Camp—due to a bad case of food poisoning.

The James children found themselves without a father—but, not for long, a couple of years later Zerelda married a man named Benjamin Simms who reportedly mistreated the kids. With divorce almost a certainty, Simms was somehow killed in a horse accident to the relief of seven-year-old Frank and three-year-old Jesse James. Their movie-worthy lives were never dull from the very beginning.

On September 25, 1855, Zerelda "tied the knot" again, but this time she married Dr. Reuben Samuel who was good to the children and gained their affections. In time, four more children were born, Archie, John, Sallie, and Fannie. The children would all help on the farm and attend school and church.

As the story goes, situated in western Missouri, the Border War with neighboring Kansas would not overlook the Samuel-James family. Raised in a Southern lifestyle their loyalties leaned in favor of the South; and raids into the area by John Brown, Jim Lane, and other abolitionists from Kansas stirred their rebel tendencies. As a result, Frank would join up with William Clarke Quantrill's guerrilla force and their raids of the border towns of Missouri and Bleeding Kansas; and later, he participated in the massacre and

Jesse James Movie

sacking of Lawrence, Kan.

Frank had just turned eighteen when he enlisted in the Confederate army on May 4, 1861. Young Jesse, only fourteen, stayed on the farm but was anxious to also join the Southern cause. One day a party of Federals rode onto the farm and, finding Jesse they demanded to know the whereabouts of Frank and Quantrill, severely bullwhipping Jesse in the process. They didn't stop there, Dr. Samuel, Jesse's beloved stepfather, was hung repeatedly for the purpose of extracting information—basically, tortured. Dr. Samuel survived but received brain damage and was eventually placed in a mental hospital in St. Joseph, Mo., where he remained until his death on March 1, 1908. This sort of historical drama went a long way in helping to foster true-to-life 1800s material for a modern-day Hollywood movie.

Jesse, now fifteen, swore vengeance on the Northern aggressors and left the Clay County farm behind to take sides and fight with the likes of "Bloody Bill" Anderson, Quantrill, and also with an independent company of partisan rangers attached to Confederate General Joseph O. Shelby.

At the Battle of Prairie Grove, Arkansas, on December 7, 1862, the James brothers rescued Gen. Shelby and he never forgot it. In the late 1860s and early 1870s when the law was "hot" on the heels of the wanted outlaws, they would occasionally visit the Shelby homestead located near Waverly, Mo., and in the Lexington *Kentucky Gazette* (quoted in the St. Louis *Republican*) it read: "There were more dainties when guests came and somehow the fire seemed brighter and bigger. But Jesse James was safe and he knew it. Shelby had announced that anyone who surrounded the house would have to take the consequences. It would have been a reckless daredevil of a detective indeed who would have dared intrude upon the Shelby homestead...Jesse made no effort to conceal his identity. He rode along the country highways and through the village streets...."

The work of the James' during the Civil War was impressive, as they fought in scores of battles and skirmishes for the Southern cause. After the War Between the States had ended, fearing retribution from Union sympathizers, extremists, and the government for their former activities during the conflict, they headed southward for the sanctuary of Texas. Finally, wanting to go home to Missouri, thinking things might have "cooled" off a bit for ex-Confederate soldiers (or guerrillas), they returned—apparently, they didn't wait long enough. As the tale is told by some, holding a white flag of peace, cease-fire, and truce, they rode into Lexington, Mo. but were suddenly fired upon by Federals. Jesse was wounded severely in the chest and suffered from it the remainder of his life—daring to think the war was at long last over for him.

From this point on, it is thought by some, Frank and Jesse James became outlaws. Lawlessness was widespread at this time due to the trouble that followed the war for a number of its participants. By some accounts, the James brothers teamed up with Cole and Jim Younger and others and robbed the Clay County Savings Association Bank of Liberty, Mo. of $72,000 on February 13, 1866. They were now "fair game" and "wanted" men—no doubt to the delight of some. It didn't stop there, they began to rob and plunder not only banks but trains. In the years that followed, the "James Gang" would help to make Missouri the "Outlaw State."

To add more fuel to the roaring fire, the James homestead at Centerville (Kearney) was attacked on January 26, 1875, by Pinkerton agents who deployed a bomb in the family fireplace which killed Jesse and Frank's nine-year-old brother and injured their mother's hand which was later amputated. Many people were outraged at the government's crude tactics.

Finally, on September 7, 1876, the James-Younger Gang attempted to "knock off" the First National Bank of Northfield, Minnesota, but the heist did not go well. During the attempted robbery Bob Younger was wounded and later died in prison; Cole and Jim Younger were also injured and captured but the James brothers would somehow escape.

A few years later while Jesse was living in St. Joseph, Mo. under the alias of Howard, a couple of his own brigands, Bob and Charlie Ford, who were seeking the reward that had been offered by Missouri Governor Thomas Crittenden, conspired to kill him. On April 3, 1882, while Jesse was standing on a chair straightening a picture which was hanging on the wall, Bob Ford got the job done

Jesse James Movie

by "plugging" him in the back and gaining the historical distinction of being considered by many as a back-shooting coward. For his efforts, Ford was given about $600 for killing the ex-rebel-turned-outlaw.

While many were outraged about the event, a number of others were relieved to hear the breaking news of the demise of the notorious Jesse James. His older brother and partner in war and crime, Frank, surrendered to authorities and appeared in court several times. At the trials, General "Jo" Shelby who the James' had rescued at the Battle of Prairie Grove, Ark., served as a character witness. At Gallatin, Mo., in August 1883 where Frank faced his most difficult charge, the murder of Frank MacMillan at a train robbery of the Rock Island Railroad at nearby Winston, Shelby also took the stand to defend the outlaw. As a result, Frank became a free man and eventually died as one in 1915 at the old Clay County farmstead where his brother was at rest.

The turbulent life and times of Jesse James opened the door to the many wild tales that followed—some of them tall. Hollywood also felt the need to—yet, again, tell the story of this American son.

The Pineville *Democrat* spread the breaking news to its readership on June 30, 1938, and thrilled the citizens of southwest Missouri, that Twentieth Century Fox had chosen Pineville to shoot a movie about the life of Jesse James to be filmed in Technicolor. The movie's screenplay was to be written by Nunnally Johnson, and star Tyrone Power as Jesse James, Henry Fonda as Frank James, and co-starring Nancy Kelly, Randolph Scott, Henry Hull, Brian Donlevy, John Carradine, Jane Darwell, and others. The movie was released in January 1939.

The movie company consisted of Henry King, director-in-chief; Robert Webb, assistant director; Sidney Bowen, financial unit manager; and George Dudley, art director. When explaining why Pineville and surrounding area was chosen for the honor, Director Henry King in an address to the Chamber of Commerce said that: "Your scenery, and locality, and general surroundings of rivers, and natural things, etc., is that which has attracted us here."

In order to relate the importance of their decision to film the movie in the area, Director King was quoted in the Pineville

MONUMENTAL TALES FORM THE OZARKS

Democrat, July 28, 1938, saying: "Pineville and your vicinity will be seen in every civilized and party civilized country in the world."

To make the town appear more like 19th century Liberty, Mo., the streets on the town square were covered with a layer of dirt; and old-fashioned wooden boardwalks, wooden awnings, hitch rails, store fronts, signs, saloon and newspaper office, etc., were constructed. The buildings received names like: "Saloon", "Dixie Belle Hotel", "Justice of the Peace", "Weekly Gazette", and "Blacksmith Shop." The town would also have people in period dress, horses, buggies, buckboards, coaches, wagons, and other things to make the motion picture look more authentic.

The company needed about 200 "extras" and people from all over were delighted and responded. "Interest is running high among the people of the Ozarks and tourists here this summer over the expected filming of the picture 'Jesse James.' Many inquires are being received by mail and by visitors in person. Some merely want to know about the picture, while others want to be in the movie or secure employment."

One local man from nearby Anderson, Dabbs Greer, landed a part in the movie and went on to star in 100 feature films, and more than 589 television shows. He is best known and remembered for his role in *Little House on the Prairie* as Reverend Alden; he is now at rest in his hometown cemetery.

About the filming and Pineville's 19th century transformation, the *Democrat* reported on August 25 that Pineville had the atmosphere of a pioneer western town with horses and vehicles assembled for inspection by the movie company. "The town was literally filled with horses and riders many of whom were dressed in costumes of 60 years ago."

Crowds of sightseers gathered around the sidelines to view the actors at work during the filming. While on the other hand, the filmmakers were trying to recreate those turbulent times in American history which had seared such a lasting mark of remembrance upon the nation. There were about seventy-five actors, technicians, operators, and assistants at the scene to "wow" the crowd. The roadways leading to the action were lined with a solid mass of cars moving in every direction. It was reported that there were about 18,000 cars said to have been counted crossing the bridge at Noel.

Besides the filming taking place at Pineville's downtown square and courthouse, scenes were also shot at a log cabin south of town, Cedar Bluff on Elk River, Crowder farm 3 miles southwest of town, train scenes at Neosho and Southwest City, and at Lake of the Ozarks where Jesse and Frank made a spectacular jump on horseback from a tall bluff into the water—the leap was made by stunt men.

The movie "Jesse James" brought thousands of needed dollars to McDonald County and surrounding area. An estimate of at least 200,000 visitors (during the time the movie was being made) brought the small hamlet and the entire area into the nation's spotlight. The movie company spent a large amount of money while in the area, as well.

Afterwards, the dirt on the town square was removed but the buildings that were created for the movie scenes were allowed to remain for a time so that curious tourists could continue to get a chance to see them—but, they too were eventually dismantled and Pineville slowly returned to its normal self. Every now and then, however, old movie buffs might run across a copy of the 1938 version of Twentieth Century Fox's "Jesse James" and wonder where it was filmed, not knowing how Hollywood once sought out the little Ozarks town of Pineville to shoot a feature film and return it to the wild and wooly 1800s.

Bibliography

Jackson, Rex T., *Hollywood and Jesse James Visited the Ozarks*, Vol. 6, No. 3, 2009, The Ozarks Reader Magazine, Neosho, Missouri.

Lexington *Kentucky Gazette* (quoted in the St. Louis *Republican*), November 9, 1898.

Pineville *Democrat*, June 30, 1938; July 28, 1938; and August 25, 1938.

Settle, Jr., William A., *Jesse James Was His Name*, University of Nebraska Press, Bison Book, 1977.

Civil War reenactment photo.

Deadly Work at the Mount Zion Church

In the northernmost fringes of the Ozarks region on a cold winter day, at a place known as Mount Zion Church near the village of Hallsville in Boone County, Missouri, a little-known battle was waged. Possibly overshadowed by more famous Missouri Civil War engagements, like the Battle of Carthage, Wilson's Creek, 1st and 2nd Newtonia, Dry Wood, Lexington, Lone Jack, Hartville, Springfield, Pilot Knob, Island Mound, and West Port, the action at the Mount Zion Church would, nevertheless, help to secure northern Missouri for the Union early in the war.

Stationed at Palmyra, Mo., Union Brigadier General Benjamin M. Prentiss (an Illinois political general who had previously served in the Mexican War, 1846-1848) received orders on the evening of December 23, 1861, to begin moving his troops the next morning to Sturgeon, which is located in northern Boone County. Gen. Prentiss, along with five troops of the 3rd Missouri Cavalry under Colonel John M. Glover, reached their destination on the evening of Dec. 26. The next day, according to the *Official Records of the Union and Confederate Armies*, Prentiss "learned that there was a concentration of rebels near the village of Hallsville."

On order to "reconnoiter...that vicinity" Prentiss sent out one of his five troops of the 3rd Missouri Cavalry under Captain James T. Howland, who proceeded to Hallsville but found no enemy forces; however, Captain Howland made the decision to press on a couple miles further where his advance guard discovered a force of

Confederates under Colonel Caleb Dorsey—an army of about 900 men. Capt. Howland attempted a hasty retreat of his company along with 9 prisoners, but was unable to escape and was overpowered by the superior numbers of the Southern force. During the process, Howland was wounded, lost his horse, and was taken hostage along with one private in his command; the rest of his Federals made a successful "beeline" back to Sturgeon arriving there at about 6 o'clock that evening.

After Gen. Prentiss learned about the incident and the Confederate strength and position he quickly ordered his five cavalry troops under Col. John M. Glover, as well as five more companies of Sharpshooters commanded by Colonel John W. Birge—about 470 in all, back to the Hallsville area; Prentiss' force left about 2 o'clock on the morning of Dec. 28th and marched the 16-mile distance in about 6 hours. Upon arrival they encountered a "company of rebels, commanded by Captain Johnson, in position to the left of the road leading from Hallsville to Mount Zion."

Two companies of Sharpshooters were then ordered "to the rear of the enemy and one of cavalry to dismount and engage them in front." The exact position of the Confederate's main force was yet unknown to Prentiss, but after some deadly work of Col. Glover's Sharpshooters—killing 5 and capturing 7, Prentiss was able to ascertain from the prisoners the enemy's position; the majority of the Southern force was posted at the Mount Zion Church and about a mile-and-a-half in advance of it.

Col. Glover's brave cavalry were ordered forward along with Col. Birge and his Sharpshooters—the cavalry dismounting to engage in battle and the Sharpshooters to the field on the right to "drive them from the woods." "The firing being heavy, these three companies," according to Gen. Prentiss, "not being able to drive the enemy form his cover, Colonel Glover, with his available force, moved in double-quick to the aid of the three companies engaged, and for half an hour longer the battle raged and became a hand-to-hand fight." By the time Col. Glover had arrived, however, Captain Boyd's Sharpshooters and Major Carrick with Company C, 3rd Missouri Cavalry, were "in the midst of the rebel camp."

Eventually, the Confederates were forces to retreat from the field

Mount Zion Church

of battle due to the deadly work of the "long range" of the Sharpshooters rifles, leaving behind about 90 horses and 105 guns in the process. The battle came to an end about 11 o'clock on the cold morning of December 28, 1861, and had lasted for about three hour's duration. Gen. Prentiss reported that "The reserve of two companies coming into action at the moment the enemy gave way, our victory was complete."

After the fighting had ended, the victors of the important conflict collected their wounded and also gathered-up the injured Confederates and "placed them in the church, and sent for farmers and friends in the vicinity to render assistance." Gen. Prentiss rounded-up his wagons, and making his "wounded as comfortable as possible," about 4 o'clock that afternoon, headed back to Sturgeon and arrived there by about 9 o'clock that night.

According to Major General H.W. Halleck, the Confederate loss was reported to be about 150 killed and wounded and 35 prisoners taken; while the Federal loss was said to have been light, 3 killed and 11 wounded. Maj. Gen. Halleck had this to say to Gen. Prentiss about the victory: "I congratulate you and your command on the affair at Mount Zion. Keep on doing so, and the rebels will soon be broken up."

About his men and their performance, Gen. Prentiss bragged that his "men behaved with coolness and daring during the engagement." Their work helped deliver a blow to the Confederate presence in northern Missouri and helped to shift the war further to the south.

About nine months later in September 1862, a regiment of Iowa troops torched the Mount Zion Church and many other buildings in the area. In 1903, however, a new Mount Zion Church was constructed at the same location. To further commemorate the bloody conflict and the fallen, a row of seven stones were placed at the site for unknown victims of the battle; and in Mount Zion Cemetery a granite marker was erected by the Sons of Confederate Veterans of the American Civil War.

The deadly work at the Mount Zion Church may not have taken "center stage" with historical distinction and famous notoriety, but its contribution to the war effort was still significant to the whole.

MONUMENTAL TALES OF THE OZARKS

Those three hours in American history once shattered the silence at the Mount Zion Church; and while it helped to determine the future of a broken nation, it also served as a field hospital where they frantically tended to the injured and wounded of the Blue and Gray who were struggling to hold on for dear life within the confines of its four walls.

Bibliography

McPherson, James M., *Battle Cry of Freedom: The Civil War Era*, Oxford University Press, New York, 1988.

Official Records of the Union and Confederate Armies, Washington: Government Printing Office, 1881.

Historic marker on the square in downtown Harrison, Arkansas.

Mountain Meadows Massacre: Wagon Train to Disaster

On the Boone County Courtyard in Harrison, Arkansas, there is a beautiful granite marker that was erected in the fall of 1955 which stands as a monument to a group of pioneer emigrants from the Ozarks. Many of these daring, adventurous souls bound for a new, promising life in California, however, never arrived.

Curious passersby can stop and read the stone's signage which was dedicated to the eternal memory of these early pioneers. Perhaps, they will learn for the first time about the horrific incident known in the annals of American and Ozarks history as the "Mountain Meadows Massacre"—one of the worst unspeakable tragedies of all times. They can ponder the historic event and dare to learn more, so that the knowledge gained can, somehow, help to prevent any like atrocities from ever happening again.

In the mid-1850s, about 140 men, women, and children from northwest Arkansas, and reportedly a few Missourians, set out for California with the notion of finding gold, cheap land, and a fresh start. The wagon train led by Alexander Francher left Caravan Spring, which is about 4 miles south of Harrison, and traveled west through the plains of Kansas and Nebraska and over the Rocky Mountains and finally into Utah Territory. While encamped at Salt Lake City, Utah, the emigrant train, with their large herd of cattle and other valuables, had gained the attention of local Mormons. At the time, tensions were running high in the religious sect as 2,500 Federal troops were en route to Utah to unseat Mormon Governor

MONUMENTAL TALES FROM THE OZARKS

Brigham Young. Past unhappy experiences in other parts of the country had brought the Mormons to this part of the West. For whatever the reason, trouble between Francher's wagon train of emigrants and the Mormons loomed ahead along the trail.

For the Mormons, it all began in the 1820s when a young farm boy in upstate New York claimed to be experiencing uncommon religious visions and revelations. Eventually, the youngster, Joseph Smith, told the tale that an angel by the name of Moroni had appeared to him and led him to some golden tablets buried nearby which contained the history of the lost tribes of Israel. The book of gold was supposedly written in an indecipherable tongue that could only be translated with the help of an angel and by wearing a giant gold breastplate that had two magic stones attached to it, which he also had to unearth. The mysterious words contained on the gold leaves supposedly became the *Book of Mormon*, which was published in 1830.

The *Book of Mormon* is believed to be as important to Mormons, or Latter-Day Saints, as the Jewish and Christian Scriptures. These are the sources, in large part, from which their faith is based.

In 1831 Joseph Smith relocated to Kirtland, Ohio, but because of persecution Smith moved his ever-growing flock of disciples to where he said, according to the *Early Days of the West* by Judge Joseph Thorp (originally published in the 1880s in the Liberty *Tribune*), "the City of Zion was to be reared and his temporal kingdom established; where his saints were to rule and reign with an iron rod till they drove out their unbelieving neighbors." This new Promised Land was to be in Jackson County, Missouri, where his converts could grow in the faith free from America's social problems and widespread materialism.

To understand more of what may have happened to the pioneers from Harrison, Ark. traveling through Mormon country in Utah, a better knowledge of Mormon history and what led them to the West, could be useful. But for many of the souls in the Francher train, precious time was running out for them.

During Joseph Smith's time in Jackson County, Mo., however, his followers helped him to establish the "Lord's Storehouse" in Independence for the purpose of trade and began publishing a newspaper called the *Evening Star*. In the paper they offered their readers Smith's revelations, which were "given to suit the times and circumstances which surrounded them, but all of them were sure to be made so as to impress their followers that they had found the Land of Canaan, and they were to drive out the heathens, or Gentiles, as they called them, and posses the land in peace."

Smith, their priest and king, made his prophesies known—that Jackson County belonged to them. It was "given to them by the Lord, and it was foolishness in them to resist and fight against God; that the temple was to be built in Independence and that saints were to be gathered from the four quarters of the globe to worship the God of Israel in the New Jerusalem."

Cool heads did not prevail and opposing sides came to blows near Westport (Kansas City) in a hand-to-hand conflict, which ended in a victory for Smith's Mormons. By and by new divine revelations from the Lord came to him that "they should destroy their ungodly enemies" and that they should "march to Independence...and complete the destruction of the place by putting the citizens to the sword and to flight."

Not to be demoralized and defeated, people came from near and far to defend against the Mormon occupation; and confronted with this overwhelming mass of wrathful humanity, Smith and his saints "agreed to lay down their arms and leave the county as soon as they could."

They put their "tails between their legs" and headed north and put down roots, for the most part, in Clay County. It was the same old "song and dance" as Smith and his disciples spread their gospel that the "country was theirs by gift of the Lord, and it was folly for them to improve their lands, they would not enjoy the fruits of their labors; that it would finally fall into the hands of the saints."

Just as before, area residents decided that the "religious fanatics" had to go. As the fever pitch rose and trouble followed the Mormons were again forced to move on—this time to Daviess County, but also into Ray, Carroll, Clinton, and Caldwell counties.

In 1836, same as before, Smith claimed they had found their Promise Land—where, of course, by divine revelation, a great temple and city would be built which was to be called: Far West. It seemed that nothing was ever learned from previous encounters with local citizens and just as in the past he preached that "anything that belonged to the unbelieving Gentiles they had a right to take wherever they found it." There followed a great amount of violence and retaliation, as a result, and many were killed—"both saints and sinners."

On October 30, 1838, tempers flared into a history-making horror that came to be known as the "Haun's Mill Massacre," which occurred at a Mormon settlement located on Shoal Creek in eastern Caldwell County a few miles south of present-day Breckenridge, Mo. At the time, as many as 30-40 Mormon families were living at the mill-site of Jacob Haun when about 250 men of the Missouri militia gathered together from neighboring counties and descended upon them. The force, under Colonel Jennings, was merciless as defenseless women and children high-tailed-it to the safety of the timberland to the south. Many of the men, however, took up position in the blacksmith shop—but, unfortunately, the spaces between the logs afforded them little or no protection from the deadly volleys of the militia's musketry. No quarter was given and the log shop became a pen of death for the huddled mass trapped inside. Even the wounded were shot down, and a ten-year-old-boy found his self at the end of a merciless muzzle of a loaded musket which blew off the top of his young head. Another man was hacked to pieces with a corn knife; and still others were mutilated while a number of women were assaulted.

When it was all said and done, about seventeen of the Haun's Mill Mormons lay dead and thirteen others were wounded. To make matters worse, the victims of the bloody massacre were thrown down into a well and covered-over with dirt and straw—and, later, despite their protests of the attack, no price was ever paid for the atrocities committed that late fall afternoon at Haun's Mill.

After this, the Mormons accepted terms of evacuation and headed for Nauvoo, Illinois, while Smith, his brother Hiram, Sidney Rigdon, Parley Pratt, Lyman Wright, and a number of others were indicted for "murder, house-burning, resisting legal process, robbery, and nearly all the crimes known to law." The group was sent to Gallatin, Mo., and then transferred to Liberty—and, eventually, ended up in Boone County where they escaped with little effort made to stop them. The fugitives rejoined the other disciples at Nauvoo where they went on to build a tabernacle and a sizeable town over the next five years. The community swelled in ranks to about fifteen thousand, but Smith was accused of advocating polygamy (plural marriage) and went so far as to publish an expose on the practice which found him, once again, in "hot water". Smith and his brother Hiram were arrested and jailed in Carthage, Illinois, where they were finally shot to death by a mob of enraged citizens.

After the demise of Joseph Smith, Brigham Young became the leader of the Mormons and in the face of great opposition in Nauvoo, relocated them to the Great Salt Lake in Utah on the western slopes of the Wasatch Mountains. In 1852 Young made the announcement that the Mormons still practiced polygamy; it is known that he had twenty-three wives. Polygamy was prohibited by Federal law in 1890.

With the Mormon population now in Utah, the stage was set for more trouble—the Francher wagon train of Ozarkians headed for California. An ungodly confrontation was at hand that would leave a nation in outrage and shock.

While Francher's group was in Cedar City, Utah, the last stop before crossing into California, the emigrants attempted to obtain some needed supplies but were turned away by the Mormons. As a result, they headed south of Cedar City into a grassy valley known as Mountain Meadows where the party decided to make camp. For several days Mormons and some of their Paiute Indian allies began to mass nearby—the wagon train was under siege.

On September 10, 1857, Francher's train was ambushed. They quickly circled the wagons for a fight and returned fire. Two other attacks were made but the Ozarkians held out; however, it was said that fifteen of their best men fell dead or were mortally wounded in the first attack.

According to an article in Harper's *Weekly*, August 8, 1859, which was written sometime afterwards, they were "Surrounded by superior numbers, and by an unseen foe...the little party stood a siege within the corral of five or seven days, sinking their wagon-

MONUMENTAL TALES FROM THE OZARKS

wheels in the ground, and during the darkness of night digging trenches, within which to shelter their wives and children...The wounded were dying of thirst; the burning brow and parched lip marked the delirium of fever...."

The day after the first attack began, on Sept. 11, 1857, one of the Mormons, John D. Lee, came to the circle of wagons holding a white flag of truce and attempted to convince them to surrender. With their ammunition nearly exhausted, the remaining emigrants put down their weapons. The Mormons told them that the Paiute Indians only wanted their property and that they, the Ozarkians, were just going to be escorted by militiamen back in the direction of Cedar City; however, having gone a mile or so, the militiamen suddenly turned on the unarmed men and killed them in cold blood—apparently, they had other plans.

Afterwards, Harper's *Weekly* reported that with the remaining women and children "some of whom had been violated by the Mormon leaders" that "helpless children clung around the knees of the savages, offering themselves as slaves; but with fiendish laughter at their cruel tortures, knives were thrust into their bodies, the scalp torn from their heads, and their throats cut from ear to ear."

In further graphic description of the aging site of the Mountain Meadows Massacre, Harper's *Weekly*, August 13, 1859, edition had this to offer: "The scene was one too horrible and sickening for language to describe. Human skeletons, disjointed bones, ghastly skulls and the hair of woman were scattered in frightful profusion over a distance of two miles."

The outrage sped across the country to nearly every newspaper and home. In the Arkansas State *Gazette* and *Democrat*, February 18, 1858, they cried for justice for their former citizens: "What will the Government do with these Mormons and Indians? Will it not send enough men to hang all the scoundrels and thieves at once, and give them the same play they gave our women and children?"

In the end, about 120 Ozarkians perished in that beautiful, but blooded Utah meadow. It would never be the same again.

Several surviving children were eventually recovered from the Mormons and brought back to their Arkansas homeland. For the rest of their lives they continued to suffer with their memories and losses.

On September 24, 1874, a few of the men were indicted for murder; however, only John D. Lee who had brought the white flag of truce into the circle of wagons that fateful day was tried and convicted. Lee was returned to Mountain Meadows Utah and shot by a firing squad on March 23, 1877—almost twenty years after the brutal massacre and other crimes.

A large overdue monument was also erected on September 15, 1990, at the Mountain Meadows site. The memorial displays the names of the victims and survivors of the horrific event. The stone marker in Harrison, Ark., and the one at Mountain Meadows, marks the beginning and the end of a long eventful journey of a group of early Ozarks pioneers that never finished their hopes and dreams of a better life in California.

About the growth of the Mormon religion first conceived by Joseph Smith, The New York *Sun*, October 10, 1883, reported that: "The church shows a membership in Utah of 127,294; number of families, 23,000; births in the past six months, 1,200 males and 1,100 females; number of children under eight years old, 37,000; number of marriages in the past six months, 339; new members, 23,040; deaths 781. The church organization embraces twelve apostles, fifty-eight patriarchs, 3,885 sureties, 3,153 high priests, 11,000 elders, 1,500 bishops and 4,400 deacons. Arizona reports a membership of 2,264. Idaho is not reported, but has double that of Arizona. Eighty-one missionaries have been appointed to go on missions to Europe and the United States."

Bibliography

Arkansas State *Gazette* and *Democrat*, February 18, 1858.
Harper's *Weekly*, August 8, 13, 1859.
Logan, Roger V., *History of Boone County, Arkansas*, Boone County Historical Railroad Society, Inc. 1994.
New York *Sun*, October 10, 1883.
Thorp, Judge Joseph, *Early Days in the West*, Liberty, Missouri, 1924.

Civil War reenactment photo.

The "Boonville Races"

Even though the Battle of Carthage, Missouri, holds the distinction of being the first significant land battle of the American Civil War, the action at Boonville, Mo., which occurred a few weeks before it, is considered to be the earliest. Less impressive in the number of troops involved and casualties compared to other great Civil War battles, the engagement at Boonville did, however, help to secure the more populated area of the state along the Missouri River from Lexington to St. Louis, as well as the fertile farming region of Missouri's upper half. According to Colonel Thomas L. Snead in *The First Year of the War in Missouri*, "The dispersion of the volunteers that were flocking to Boonville to fight under Price for Missouri and the South extended Lyon's conquest at once to the borders of Iowa, closed all the avenues by which the Southern men of North Missouri could get to Price and Jackson, made the Missouri River a Federal highway from its source to its mouth, and put an end to Price's hope of holding the rich and friendly counties in the vicinity of Lexington till the Confederacy could send an army to his support, and arms and supplies for the men whom he was concentrating there." For the Southern troops under Missouri Governor Claiborne Fox Jackson and Major General Sterling Price, their retreat from that battleground to the South became known by some as the "Boonville Races."

After the Union's capture of the St. Louis Arsenal in May 1861, which helped to catapult Missouri into civil war, forces were being mustered together on both sides of the argument. Since Gen. Price had taken ill and could not take to the field and command the State

Guards at this time, he was forced to send—in his stead, Colonel John S. Marmaduke who was a West Pointer and a nephew of Gov. Jackson. Col. Marmaduke was ordered to the Boonville area with "about eight hundred 'barefoot Rebel militia,' nucleus of the State Guards army," according to *Battles and Biographies of Missourians* by W.L. Webb, and they were "armed with Derringer pocket pistols, family fowling pieces, squirrel rifles, old flint-locks, long knives made of files which had been beaten into shape by blacksmiths," and so on.

On the other hand, Brigadier General Nathaniel Lyon and his Union troops consisted of the "light battery, under Captain Totten, Second Artillery; Company B, Second Infantry...; two companies of recruits for the regular service, under Lieut. W.L. Lothrop, Fourth Artillery; First Regiment Missouri Volunteers, under Col. F.P. Blair, jr.; nine companies Second Regiment Missouri Volunteers, under Col. Henry Boernstein,"—about 1,700 men in all. Lyon's forces boarded some riverboats and steamed upriver to Jefferson City, arriving there on June 15, 1861, at about 2 o'clock in the afternoon.

After discovering that the Southern forces of Gov. Jackson and Gen. Price had vacated the area and moved their troops to Boonville, Lyon left Boernstein at Jefferson City with three companies of his regiment and continued his pursuit of the enemy the next day further upriver making about 15 miles; the following day, June 17, 1861, Lyon steamed ahead about 8 miles from Boonville where he left an "8-inch howitzer, with an artillery party and Captain Richardson's company, First Missouri Volunteers, as guard to the three boats," and the rest advanced in search of the enemy camp.

Meanwhile, Col. Marmaduke was appealing to Gov. Jackson that an engagement at this point with Lyon's better prepared army might be unwise, but the commander-in-chief ordered him to prepare for conflict. It made little difference to Gen. Lyon as his Federals were making ready to attack, and according to his report in the *Official Records of the Union and Confederate Armies* to General George B. McClellan dated June 30, 1861, he wrote: "After about two miles' march we met an advanced party of the rebel forces, which opened fire upon us, but soon fell back. To meet this resistance, the skirmishers already forward were collected to the right of our road. Company B, Second Infantry, was thrown out to the left, and opened fire. Two pieces of Captain Totten's battery were brought into play, and several shots fired."

After this, Lyon deployed Lieutenant Lothrop's forces of Captain Yates' Company H, Missouri Volunteers, and additional troops of the Third Missouri Volunteers to the right side of the road. About a mile ahead they again encountered Marmaduke's militia, and Lyon's left flank was further reinforced by the First Missouri Volunteers, Company B, under Captain Maurice. Lyon reported in the *Official Records* that "The enemy, having shelter of a house (owned by Wm. M. Adam) and a thicket of wood behind it, held their position for a while, during which time our approach brought us on to high open ground, and here most of our casualties occurred."

Capt. Totten's big guns pounded the Southerners while the Federals continued to inch their left and right flanks forward, which eventually began to force Marmaduke's men to fall back. The retiring Confederates, according to Lyon, "took advantage of sundry points to deliver a fire and continue retreating."

W.L. Webb in giving credit to the outgunned, inexperienced, untrained farm boys that made up a large part of the State Guards wrote that they "fought doggedly and stood their ground longer than generalship would have permitted, but they were not properly officered and didn't know how to come off the field. They had failed to make good the common boast that 'one Missourian could whip three Yankees.' " And, although the battle turned into a hurried retreat, or rout some called the Boonville Races, the Union forces of Gen. Lyon was not able to "arrest the insurgents"—something he would have, no doubt, enjoyed accomplishing.

Upon entering the city, citizens asked Lyon not to plunder the town; he promised not to as long as there was no opposition to his arrival and occupation of it. Lyon and his men solidified this early Union victory by entering the enemy camp located near the Missouri River and capturing two 6-pound iron cannons and "about 500 stand of arms of all sorts" and "about 60 prisoners," which he released on "oath to obey the laws of the General Government and not to oppose it during the present civil troubles." On the lower side of Boonville, they also discovered that the fairgrounds had been utilized as an arsenal, and they recovered a large amount of "old rusty arms and cartridges" to complete the town's Union takeover and occupation.

The State Guards licked their wounds and regrouped with recovering-from-his-sickness Gen. Price and high-tailed-it to southwest Missouri and the town of Lamar. On July 15, 1861, Gov. Jackson and Gen. Price returned the favor at Carthage and routed Union forces under the command of Colonel Franz Sigel, Third Missouri Infantry, and proceeded to McDonald County and Cowskin Prairie where they would train and mass for the upcoming Battle of Wilson's Creek on August 10, 1861, near Springfield.

The Confederates would go on to win the Battle of Wilson's Creek, as well; while Gen. Lyon would lose his life. The brothers that clashed at this early land battle known as the Boonville Races went on speedily to the many other monumental engagements that followed on its heels.

The "Boonville Races"

Bibliography

Official Records of the Union and Confederate Armies, Washington: Government Printing Office, 1881.

Snead, Thomas L., *The First Year of the War in Missouri*, Battles and Leaders of the Civil War, The Century Company, 1887.

Webb, W. L., *Battles and Biographies of Missourians* or *The Civil War Period of Our State*, Hudson-Kimberly Publishing Company, Kansas City, Missouri, 1900.

The Jacob Wolf House in Norfork, Arkansas.

Major Jacob Wolf House: Arkansas' Oldest Public Building

During the western expansion of America after 1765, many pioneers heading to the West came from the hill country of Kentucky and Tennessee and settled in the Ozarks region. The area being, for the most part, from the Missouri River on the northern reaches to the Arkansas River at the southern border; the eastern edge of the Ozarks is considered to be the Mississippi River, however, some contend parts of southwestern Illinois should be included; in the west, a small corner of southeastern Kansas and a sizeable area of northeastern Oklahoma make up that portion of the Ozarks region.

For the early pioneers, the rugged hills and vales of the Ozarks contained an abundance of hardwoods and pine forests which supplied the logs and building materials to construct their homes and outbuildings. The log cabin became the characteristic dwelling-choice of the frontier; and by the 19th century, log cabins symbolized the pioneer spirit that had sweep across the New World—before this time Native Americans utilized other methods.

The log cabin was first introduced in 1658 in the Delaware River Valley by early Swedish settlers who had brought the method of log construction to America from northern Europe. Many well-known figures like Abraham Lincoln, Ulysses S. Grant, and George Washington Carver were born in a log cabin. Most frontier schools and other important structures were also made of logs during this period.

MONUMENTAL TALES FROM THE OZARKS

Pioneers would cut and fell trees in order to clear land and build their cabins. The logs would be debarked, in most cases, or hewn square to remove the outer wood, leaving the more desirable, durable heartwood. The logs would be laid horizontally and jointed (notched) at the corners—no nails were used. Then, the remaining gaps between the logs would be chinked with mud, clay, or other readily available native materials to seal out the weather and other unwanted guests; a fireplace was also a necessary addition to the frontier cabin, which was generally made of stone or brick and used for heating and cooking.

As time passed, almost every community in the Ozarks region had a sawmill or two; it was a gathering place where Ozarkians could get their lumber sawed and their flour and feed ground. Settlers used crosscut saws and axes to fell trees, and dragged and "snaked" the logs overland with horses and pulled wagons and used the many streams and rivers that wind and twist through the hills and hollows to get the logs to the mills. They utilized the trunks for saw logs and the tops for firewood, which they burned to carry them through the cold winter months.

A prime example of an early log cabin was built on a hillside overlooking the White River in present-day Norfork, Arkansas by Jacob Wolf. The two-story, hand-hewn, dogtrot log cabin known as the Jacob Wolf House is believed to be the oldest public structure in the state. Historians, amateur history buffs, and travelers who happen on to the Jacob Wolf House on Highway 5 in Baxter County will find ample inspiration on an educational journey back into the past—at least while the old icon still stands. In the pictorial book of photos by David Fitzgerald and text by Clay Anderson titled *Portrait of the Ozarks*, it shows the great-great-grandniece, Helen Chapman, standing in front of the Jacob Wolf House when she used to conduct guided tours of the property. The home and site has continued over-the-years thanks to the Wolf House Memorial Foundation, Inc. and by many other concerned supporters.

Jacob Wolf was born in North Carolina in 1786, and lived in Kentucky before finally moving to what was then Arkansas Territory in the early 1820s. He became an Indian agent and traded goods and supplies to Native Americans for buffalo hides, deer skins, and other things while traveling the White River in the Ozarks' wild, untamed wilderness. Wolf was commissioned a major in the 7th Regiment of the Arkansas Territorial Militia on December 3, 1825, and served as a territorial legislator from 1827 to 1835. He endeavored to create a bustling town known as "Izard Court House" and then "Liberty," after donating land in 1829 to build the first permanent territorial courthouse (the Wolf House) in Izard County, which was named after George Izard who was governor of Arkansas; the site later became part of Baxter County when Arkansas finally became a state in 1836 and county lines were established.

United States President John Quincy Adams appointed George Izard as the second governor of Arkansas territory; James Miller was its first governor. George Izard was born in October 1776 in Richmond, England, but relocated to France in 1777. Izard went to school and stayed in France until 1789. He came to America and attended the Columbia College in New York, and went on to, among other things, receive a commission during the War of 1812 as a brevet major general, where he had a command on the United States and Canadian border. George Izard remained the governor of Arkansas until he died in Little Rock in 1828.

Dr. David Staley of the University of Arkansas studied the Jacob Wolf House yellow pine logs growth-rings and determined that they were probably cut and left to cure sometime between 1825 and 1826. The construction date of the log courthouse, which is believed to be 1829, also corresponded with the Izard County territorial legislation time-frame—further confirmation of the construction date. The original lime for building the fireplaces, foundation, and log chinking came from grinding mussel shells taken from the river.

County government held regular sessions and circuit court during the time the structure served as the "seat of justice," until the territorial legislature voted to relocate the county seat to Atkins in 1835. During the time it served as a courthouse, people came from far and wide and families would camp out on the grounds of the Wolf House. Sessions often lasted several days, and to kill time there were shooting contests, wrestling competition, tomahawk tossing, and a host of other things. After the county seat was relocated Major Wolf had the property deeded back to his self. It then became his home where he, widowed twice, raised sixteen children in the house that the first Mrs. Wolf affectionately called "the mansion." There were grand weddings, cotillions, birthdays, and many other memorable events held in the home and on the grounds in its heyday.

Wolf established a ferry across the river to accommodate those who arrived by wagon, canoe, keelboat, and steam-powered riverboats; as it was the headwaters of navigation. Thousands passed-by or stopped to trade at Wolf's store, blacksmith shop, and woodworking shop. There was also a post office where John P. Houston, brother of legendary Sam Houston, served as the county clerk. One of the home's most famous visitors, however, was Davy Crockett who was eventually killed and mutilated in Texas at the Alamo. The post office continued to operate until the Civil War broke out in 1861; when a Union officer tried to commandeer the house, Major Wolf attacked him with a cane and was rewarded with a year's imprisonment at Batesville, Ark.

Jacob Wolf became well-known to many and died in the Wolf House on January 1, 1863, at the age of 77. He left behind a large family of friends and relatives.

The interpretive signs and other support found at the site were funded in part by the Arkansas Humanities Council, the Department of Arkansas Heritage, the Wolf House Memorial Foundation, and the Baxter County Judge's office. The house is listed on the National Register of Historic Places. It is open to the public for self-guided walking tours.

The spectacular view from the Wolf House porch overlooking the White River and the scenic Ozarks surroundings, offers up to history-hungry visitors a unique insight back into America's pioneering past. The colorful tales stored within the home's walls, the sounds of a coming riverboat steamer's bell, the courtyard noise of human activity and contribution, or the clank, clank on the anvil of the blacksmith's hammer, may escape us now, but only if we have no sense of wonder or imagination to revisit it in the mind's eye.

Bibliography

Anderson, Clay, *Portrait of the Ozarks*, (photos by David Fitzgerald), Graphic Arts Center Publishing, Portland, Oregon, 1995.

Deane, Ernie, *Ozarks Country*, The Ozarks Mountaineer, Kirbyville, Missouri, 1978; *Arkansas Place Names*, The Ozarks Mountaineer, Branson, Missouri, 1986.

Jackson, Rex T., *Jacob Wolf House; Arkansas' Oldest Public Structure*, Vol. 2, No. 1, 2005, The Ozarks Reader Magazine, Neosho, Missouri.

Wolf House, Interpretive Signage, Norfork, Arkansas.

Historic marker near Osceola, Missouri.

Destruction of Osceola and the Sauk River Camp

Early in the American Civil War a number of things helped to encourage Southern recruitment in Missouri, like President Abraham Lincoln's calling up of 75,000 troops, and Lyon's capture of the St. Louis Arsenal where several citizens were killed—men, women, and children. Another incident would also help to compel thousands of Missourians to join the Southern cause, the destruction of Osceola, Missouri and more death.

In order to remember these Civil War citizen-soldiers, just north of the town square in Nevada, Mo., on the front lawn of the old Vernon County Jail, an historic marker erected in 2001 by the Missouri Division Sons of Confederate Veterans, reads: "This monument is respectfully dedicated to the men of the Missouri State Guard. The legally established militia of the state, who first took up arms in 1861, and, marching and fighting under the Blue Flag of their beloved Missouri did their whole duty as God gave them light to see that duty, and sacrificed everything but honor in the defense of their states sovereignty and the cause of constitutional rights."

In nearby Fort Scott, Kansas, the mindset of the Union forces was no less determined. In the *Official Records of the Union and Confederate Armies*, Brigadier General James H. Lane writes to the commander at Fort Leavenworth on August 25, 1861, and says: "Our little force will be actively employed to defend Kansas and confuse Missourians. But, sir, I assure you that Fort Leavenworth and Kansas should be defended from this point, and the idea of holding artillery to rust at Fort Leavenworth does not strike me with any favor. I hope the first troops forwarded will bring down artillery that can be used to some purpose...

"Can you not send us re-enforcements; with it, we could play hell with Missouri in a few days."

Whether or not Union Brig. Gen. Lane was able to get his reinforcements or artillery guns from Fort Leavenworth, is unclear, however, only a few days later—true to his word, on September 22, 1861, Lane played "hell with Missouri" and attacked Osceola in St. Clair County.

In an attempt to remember the actions in the area during those turbulent years of the Civil War, on a bluff overlooking the Sauk (Sac) and Osage River confluence is a beautiful stone marker. This scenic overlook just south of Osceola makes it hard to imagine that this eye-popping Ozarks site could have ever participated in any such bloody, national conflict, and that afterwards, multitudes gathered here to join in the fight.

The very reason for their interest in being recruited was recorded in the *Official Records* on September 24, 1861, by Brig. Gen. Lane to Major General Fremont, Commanding the Western Department: "My brigade is now marching to this point from Osceola, where I have been on a forced march, expecting to cut off the enemy's train of ammunition. The enemy ambushed the approaches to the town, and after being driven from them by the advance under Colonels [James] Montgomery and [William] Weer, they took refuge in the buildings of the town to annoy us. We were compelled to shell them out, and in doing so the place was burned to ashes, with an immense amount of stores of all descriptions. There were 15 to 20 of them killed and wounded; we lost none."

Another report in the *Official Records* by B. Rush Plumly to Colonel Thomas A. Scott, Assistant Secretary of War, dated October 3, 1861, offers a slightly different account: "Lane chased Rains into Osceola, and was compelled to shell the place to dislodge the rebels. In doing so he burned the town and destroyed large stores of the rebels, of which the town was the depot. Killed 50 rebels without losing a man."

Maybe a little worried that Maj. Gen. Fremont might not have approved of his attack and destruction of Osceola, Brig. Gen. Lane writes to him again on Sept. 24, 1861, and says: "I hope, as you have now opened communication with me, to hear from you frequently. I trust you will approve the march on Osceola and its destruction. It was the depot of the traitors for Southwestern Missouri."

The importance of the town of Osceola was due in large part to its location situated at the headwaters of river navigation, and as a shipping-point for goods from southwest Missouri and Indian Territory (Oklahoma) and places beyond; tons of lead were transported to Osceola from Granby, Mo., and then on to St. Louis, Mo., for instance.

About the "fallout" of Osceola's fate, Wiley Britton, a Federal soldier who wrote *The Civil War on the Border*, and was quoted by W.L. Webb in his book *Battles and Biographies of Missourians*, wrote: "In destroying the town, Gen. Lane seemed to be unconscious of the fact that his conduct would be just excuse for retaliation, and that it might possibly come with interest...Perhaps upwards of one-third of the people of St. Clair County were Unionists, and many of the men were in the Federal army; some, too, in Kansas regiments. Gen. Lane destroyed and appropriated their property with the same recklessness that he did the property of the Secessionists."

A few weeks later after the destruction of Osceola, Confederate Major General Sterling Price (Old Pap), would wisely establish a recruitment camp at the confluence of the Sauk and Osage Rivers near Osceola and from October through December, 1861, 12,000 men gathered to offer their services to the South: about 8,000 joined Gen. Price in the Confederate army; 2,000 were mustered into the Missouri State Guard, and the rest went on to wage a guerrilla war in the area.

Prior to this, the Missouri State Guard had been victorious at the battles of Carthage, Wilson's Creek (Oak Hills), Lexington, and Dry Wood. Before long, however, on March 7-8, 1862, Gen. Price's recruits would participate in the bloody Battle of Pea Ridge, fought near Pea Ridge, Arkansas. They would also fight in battles east of the Mississippi River, and with Price in his final Missouri plunge in

1864 at: Pilot Knob, Westport (Kansas City), Mine Creek (Kansas), and Newtonia.

Fifteen generals were produced from among the ranks: John S. Bowen, John Clark, John Clark Jr., Francis M. Cocrell, Basil Duke, Daniel Frost, Martin Green, Henry Little, James Major, John M. Marmaduke, M.M. Parsons, James Rains, William Slack, Joseph O. Shelby, and Sterling Price.

Citizen-soldiers fought bravely for many and various reasons and took the side they felt compelled to defend. For some, however, they made their choice after the attack, plunder, and burning of Osceola.

Bibliography

Webb, W. L., *Battles and Biographies of Missourians* or *The Civil War Period of Our State*, Hudson-Kimberly Publishing Company, Kansas City, Missouri, 1900.

Official Records of the Union and Confederate Armies, Washington: Government Printing Office, 1881.

Sauk River Camp Historic Marker, Osceola, Missouri.

Reproduction gallows at Fort Smith Historic Site in Fort Smith, Arkansas.

Shades of Fort Smith

Overlooking the Arkansas and Poteau river confluence about fifty feet above the mixing waters, a site was chosen to build a fort—one of several in a line that stretched from Fort Snelling, Minnesota, through America's heartland. The need to establish a fort in west-central Arkansas in the southern reaches of the Ozarks region and along the border with Indian Territory (Oklahoma) was a result of western expansion and the relocation of Eastern Native American tribes to the West.

The original site of Fort Smith, Arkansas was first known as Belle Point and was appointed for selection on July 30, 1817, by Acting Secretary of War Richard Graham. Some of its first functions was the preservation of peace between the Osage and Cherokee Indians and to keep settlers from trespassing into Indian Territory, which they did on many occasions, stealing horses, hunting buffalo—taking only their hides and tallow, squatting, pushing "rot gut" whiskey, and other things.

By the 1830s, Belle Point had become the busiest center of activity in the Southwest frontier. The station's log and native rock structures, palisade walls, and garrison, on the point above the two rivers, soon commanded respect on the border of the Indian Nations. The scenic Ozarks area around Belle Point was described by Thomas Nuttall, a student of natural science, and in his *A Journal of Travels into the Arkansas Territory during the Year 1819* published in 1905, he writes: "Our route was continued through prairies, occasionally divided by sombre belts of timber, which serve to mark the course of rivulets. These vast plains, beautiful almost as the fancied Elysium, were now enameled with innumerable flowers, among the most splendid of which were the azure larkspur...fragrant phloxes, and the purple psilotria. Serene and charming as the blissful regions of fancy, nothing here appeared to exist but what contributes to harmony."

Belle Point continued until 1824, and during that time in the fort's service soldiers kept an eye on warring Indian tribes fighting over hunting grounds and territory; and they also helped to protect American citizens. In late February 1839, however, construction on a second more impressive Fort Smith had begun at its new location east, but next to the original Belle Point fort. It would also rise up close to the new town platted by John Rogers in 1838, also named Fort Smith.

The new Fort Smith, built mainly of brick, would serve as a supply depot for provisions of food, supplies, and military equipment received mostly from riverboat steamers destine for such Southwest outposts as: Fort Gibson, Fort Towson, Fort Wayne, Cantonment Belnap, and Camp Mason, Holmes, and Washita in Indian Territory. In the Fort Smith *Herald*, July 6, 1850, it had this to say about the condition and strength of the fort: "The public buildings, for Military Purposes, at this place, are the largest, and best buildings on the Western Frontier...A more healthy place for troops we venture to say, is not to be found in the United States than Fort Smith."

Soldiers at Fort Smith would fall into rank at daybreak. They would make their beds, sweep and have everything in order for inspection less than a half hour after morning reveille. After breakfast, soldiers would clean their weapons and generally get themselves prepared for nine o'clock parade on the grounds. The nation's colors would be raised and the "Star Spangled Banner" would be played, while marching in review. They would be posted on guard or, for the rest of the day clean the post, repair or maintain the garrison, or whatever was needed. Soldiers would care for horses, cut wood, do yard work or any other necessary chore. Supper was served at one o'clock; the flag lowered at sunset; and final roll call was taken at nine o'clock. By nine-thirty it was time

Shades of Fort Smith

for bed and taps were made by the drum.

By 1858, the fort served as a mail route for the Overland Mail that merged there from Memphis, Tennessee, and St. Louis, Missouri. That fall, it became a major stop for the Butterfield Overland Mail Stagecoach Route which began in Tipton, Mo. (the end of the rail line), and ran southwest to El Paso, Texas, and on to San Francisco, California—a total of about 2,800 miles that took fifteen and one-half bone-jarring days to travel.

When the call for secession approached during the American Civil War (1861-1865), state troops seized old Belle Point and Fort Smith for its precious strategic location, military stores, and subsistence. After the ordinance of secession from the Union was adopted at a convention in Little Rock, Ark., and the fort was seized, Fort Smith quickly became a useful command post for Confederate troops guarding the northwest approach to Arkansas, Texas, and Louisiana. It was here that the Confederacy staged campaigns for the battles that were waged at Cane Hill, Prairie Grove, Pea Ridge, southwest Missouri, Indian Territory, and other places.

However, on September 1, 1863, Union forces under General James G. Blunt took possession of Fort Smith, and according to a report made by Gen. Blunt to General John M. Schofield on September 3, 1863, in the *Official Records of the Union and Confederate Armies*, he was happy to say that they raised the "stars and stripes to the breeze" over Fort Smith.

Problems never ceased, and the necessity of the fort and its purpose never diminished. In *The American Indian as Participant in the Civil War* author Annie Heloise Abel writes: "...the year 1863 proved critical...Around Fort Smith, in Arkansas, things were...bad. People were clamoring for protection against marauders, some were wanting only the opportunity to move themselves and their effects far away out of reach of danger, others were demanding that the unionists be cleaned out just as secessionists had, in some cases, been."

By 1870, however, only five years after the end of the Civil War, the War Department decided to abandon the post because of its waning usefulness. By the end of 1871, Fort Smith had been permanently vacated by the military. The once bustling hub of activity fell silent, musketry and cannon-fire was no longer heard, nor roll call, but Fort Smith would not stand idle or turn its back on still more colorful history. The same year the military evacuated the fort, the United States Court of the Western District of Arkansas was moved to Fort Smith in order to deal with the blossoming lawlessness that followed the war—especially in Indian Territory. The courtroom and jail occupied the old military barracks, and President Ulysses S. Grant appointed Isaac C. Parker who became known as the "Hanging Judge" to the district.

Judge Isaac C. Parker arrived with his family to Fort Smith on May 2, 1875. A few days later he began his twenty-one year jurisdiction, where he would employ a large number of U.S. marshals. Parker's red, white, and black marshals would patrol his district, including Indian Territory, and face some of the worst rough and tough characters to ever walk the earth. Before long, the need to erect a scaffold was apparent, due to the many hombres sentenced to hang.

A reporter with the St. Louis *Republican* wrote on September 4, 1875, about the coming of Parker's gallows and the construction of it at the post which carried a sign "The Gates of Hell," saying that: "The structure is built of rough timbers. The crossbeam is a stout piece of hewed oak, supported on two upright posts, very strongly braced. The platform is about seven feet from the ground. The distance between the supporting posts is about twelve feet, giving nearly two feet space for the fall of each victim...an iron trigger bar which passes up through a place provided in the trap doors and is secured by a knee in a strong iron lever about three feet long, well secured on the facing of the platform floor. By a movement of this lever back, the trigger bar which holds the trap in position is released and the doors drop down. On this door the condemned men will stand. Six ropes at this moment are tied over the beam, and six bags of sand of 200 pounds in weight each have been thrice dropped to test the further working of this awful enginery of death."

From 1875 to 1896, crowds of death-loving spectators thronged to Parker's annual main attraction to witness the swinging of not just a few poor souls on their way to their eternal destiny. The mass executions became one of the Southwest frontier's most popular events. One of the trials during Judge Parker's reign at Fort Smith that also excited the locals was the trial of "Belle Starr," or Myra Belle Shirley, who was found guilty of horse theft and sentenced to one year in prison to be served in Detroit, Michigan at the House of Corrections. The jail cell beneath Parker's courtroom, however, became known as the "Hell on the Border," and was a place not many cared to be incarcerated at.

The western frontier was a wild, wooly, and rugged place during the 19th century. It was a haunt and an "owl-hoot trail" for many outlaws, renegades, and desperados on the run, like John Wesley Hardin, Bill Miner, William M. "Bill" Doolin, Roy "Arkansas Tom" Daugherty, Henry Starr, Bill, Bob, Grat, and Emmett Dalton, and many others. No place in the West was more crime-ridden than the Indian Nations, where many of these gun slinging hombres roamed at will and enjoyed their freedom to defy the government and commit a multitude of heinous crimes. One infamous individual of bad repute who enjoyed the liberty of breaking the law was a man named Crawford Goldsby, who became one of Judge Parker's gallows victims. Goldsby, also known as "Cherokee Bill" (some sources include the name "Cherokee Kid"), was born in Fort Concho, Texas on February 8, 1876. Reportedly, Cherokee Bill was part African American, white, Mexican, and Cherokee, and some conclude that he was part Sioux and Cherokee, but whatever the case, he was a mixed-blood American full of the Old Nick.

Cherokee Bill moved to Indian Territory and by 1894 he had hooked-up with a few other lawless public enemies and began his crime spree of robbery and murder. Judge Parker eventually issued a reward for him—dead or alive, and before long in January 1895, he was captured by some of the judge's marshals. He was taken to Fort Smith to await trial where he was convicted of murder and given the death penalty.

On July 26, 1895, Cherokee Bill masterminded a daring jailbreak by somehow obtaining a gun from a trustee at the prison. In the attempt, a firefight took place which scored Cherokee Bill yet another victim to add to his list of killings. Outlaw Henry Starr, who was also incarcerated at Parker's jail, aided the guards by going in and convincing Cherokee Bill to surrender his firearm—which he did; afterwards, he received a double sentence. Judge Parker dubbed him a "blood thirsty mad dog who killed for the love of killing." Starr's role in the matter helped to later gain him his freedom.

Appeals were denied and Cherokee Bill's execution was set. The 20-year-old spent his final days playing poker with other inmates through the bars of his cell; his last game was with Charley Smith and Henry Starr. In the Fort Smith *Elevator*, March 20, 1896, it had this to report about the hours leading up to the hanging of Cherokee Bill, which took place on March 17, 1896, before hundreds of curious onlookers: "The usual noise and hubbub that is always heard within the big iron cage that surrounds the cells was noticeably lacking this morning. Cherokee Bill's fellow-prisoners, many of them under sentence of death, seemed to be impressed with the solemnity of the occasion, and an air of subdued quiet pervaded the jail....

"...the corridor in front of the Cherokee's cell was crowded with newspaper representatives, deputy marshals and other privileged individuals, all taking note of every passing incident....

"From the time he killed [the jailer]...up to the day of his execution he has been kept shackled and confined in his cell...."

Finally, when the time had arrived, he was led to Parker's sturdy gallows, climbed the thirteen steps and waited. Reportedly, when asked about whether or not he wanted any last words before his execution, he said: "I came here to die, not to make a speech." The iron lever was pulled and he fell through the trap door and into eternity.

When Judge Parker, the "hanging judge of Fort Smith" died on November 17, 1896, he had hanged a total of eighty-eight men during his service to the United States Court of the Western District of Arkansas. The word of his demise spread like wildfire in the prison and there was cause for great rejoicing among the relieved inmates.

In 1961, the United States Congress moved to establish Fort Smith as a National Historic Site where visitors could see the barracks, courthouse, jail, reproduction gallows, Belle Point site,

Choctaw territory marker, and the historic overlook and crossing of the "Trail of Tears." The monumental contributions of Fort Smith continues to remind the nation of its roots and early settlement, not just for the law abiding but also for those who didn't quite measure up to America's moral standards.

Bibliography

Abel, Annie Heloise, *The American Indian as Participant in the Civil War*, Arthur H. Clark Company, Cleveland, 1919.

Bearss, Edwin C., and Gibson, A.M., *Fort Smith: Gibraltar on the Arkansas*, University of Oklahoma Press, Norman, Oklahoma, 1969.

Fort Smith *Elevator*, March 20, 1896.

Fort Smith *Herald*, July 5, 1850.

Harman, S. W., *Hell on the Border: He Hanged Eighty-Eight Men*, Phoenix Publishing Company, Fort Smith, 1898.

McNab, Chris, *Gunfighters: The Outlaws and Their Weapons*, Thunder Bay Press, San Diego, California, 2005.

Nuttal, Thomas, *A Journal of Travels into the Arkansas Territory during the Year 1819*, 1905.

Official Records of the Union and Confederate Armies, Washington: Government Printing Office, 1881.

St. Louis *Republican*, September 4, 1875.

Young, Richard and Judy Dockery, *Outlaw Tales: Legends, Myths, and Folklore from America's Middle Border*, August House, Inc., Little Rock, Arkansas, 1992.

Alley Mill and Spring located near Eminence, Missouri.

Mills, Resorts, and Spas

When early mountaineers settled in the hills and valleys of the untamed Ozarks, they made quick use of its abundance and bounty—timber, wildlife, fruits and nuts, and water. The beauty that they discovered is common today in jigsaw puzzles, postcards, calendars, paintings, newspapers, books, and magazines. It didn't take long before these industrious, pioneering individuals realized the potential of the region's rivers, streams, and springs as a source of power and energy.

During the 1800s and early 1900s, many water-powered mills were constructed to harness the seemingly endless, free power of Ozarks water. They were created, for the most part, to grind corn and wheat and to mill lumber. These mills commonly used "overshot" or "undershot" wheels for power, which was determined by the lay of the land and the source of the water. Dams were often constructed to back up water to form a pond or water reserve which could be diverted to the mill race and power an undershot wheel; on the other hand, an overshot wheel utilized water from a hillside spring above the mill which was then carried to the top of the wheel to power it.

Preferably, mills that used one buhr stone for flour and one for cornmeal was best, since corn leaves an oily residue that clings to the stone's surface. The distance between the grinding stones needed to be closely monitored, hence, the old saying: "Keep your nose to the grindstone." The stone's surface was called the "land" and the grooves that were cut into it were known as "furrows."

MONUMENTAL TALES FROM THE OZARKS

Many settlements sprang up around watermills, and people would travel from miles around to bring their wagon loads of grain or logs to be ground into meal or sawn into needed lumber. The millers would generally charge a fee or take a percentage of the finished product for doing the job.

Many early pioneers also made use of the abundant water in nearby creeks and springs to have their "wash day." Families would load up the dirty laundry into a horse-drawn wagon and head for the water. Often it became a perfect chance to pack a picnic lunch to enjoy while the clothes were drying on a makeshift clothesline strung between trees.

The importance of water has generated much human activity throughout American history. An excellent example of this is located a few miles west of Eminence, Missouri, in an area well-suited to watermills: the Alley Spring Roller Mill; a grist mill that used rollers instead of millstones. A place where anyone interested in the past and how our forerunners solved and overcome the obstacles of power and energy will learn much about their ingenuity and practicability.

The nearby town of Eminence, located in Shannon County, was first established to the north of the Current River in 1841; however, the town was destroyed and left in ruins as a result of the American Civil War (1861-1865). In 1868, Eminence was relocated and laid out on Jack's Fork of the Current River. The first copper mine in Missouri was founded near Eminence by Joseph Slater in 1837. Between 1880 and 1920, thousands of acres of forest were harvested in the region by large commercial lumber companies. The area is rich in water resources and a number of popular state parks have been created, such as: Alley Spring and Mill, Round Spring, Blue Spring, Ebb-and-Flow Spring, Welch Spring, and Horse Hollow. The Ozark National Scenic Riverways of the United States Department of the Interior National Park Service offers fishing, floating, boating, camping, hiking, sightseeing, and a host of other things.

At a spring once known as Mammoth Spring and then Barksdale Spring, where a whopping 81 million gallons of water flows out daily out of a funnel-shaped basin that is about 32-feet deep, a mill

Mills, Resorts, and Spas

was constructed as early as 1868. Before long a thriving community began to grow which included a blacksmith shop, general store, school, and a post office. The village name, Alley, was later adopted from a prominent local miller, John Alley.

The current Alley Mill was built in 1894 by George Washington McCaskill. It was first painted white and trimmed in green but was eventually repainted red. John Knotts became the owner of the mill in 1902 and Conrad Hug in 1912; Hug turned the hamlet of Alley into one of the first resorts in Missouri known as Crystal Spring Town Site.

As the timber in the area became depleted, lumber milling at Alley ceased, for the most part, by 1919. With the advent of electricity and other modern innovations, and because the Alley roller-type mill was more suited to the production of wheat flour in an area where mostly corn was grown, the mill fell silent and the village followed suit—the lively, human sounds of picnics, dances, and games also came to an end.

By the mid-1920s, however, conservation efforts in the area had begun. In 1969, Alley Spring and Mill became part of the Ozark National Scenic Riverways. Alley Mill, and the many other Ozark mills, are monuments to the past and a reminder of early mountaineers that helped to herald in a new way of life as they harnessed the power of water—a simple, but effective form of energy.

Another popular use of the abundant resource of water during the western expansion and early pioneer times was resorts and spas. During the 1800s much of the civilized world had not yet reached the Ozarks region. Modern medical science was still in its infancy and people turned to whatever was available or popular when it came to their health. One of the early forms of treatment was the use of mineral waters which flowed from the numerous springs and wells.

Mineral waters were used for drinking and bathing from ancient times. In biblical times it was believed that mineral water could purify and renew the soul; and during the "golden age" of the resort and spa in the 19th century, promoters used this as a means of outlandish claims of healing—and believers came by the thousands for the promised, miracle cures.

The Greeks valued mineral springs and by 300 A.D. there were about eight hundred bathhouses in Rome, Italy. The term "spa" is taken from a town in Belgium, in Liege Province, which is also well-known for its mineral baths.

Natural Ozark mineral water is categorized as: muriatic (containing salt); alkaline; sulfatic; and chalybeate (containing iron). It occurs as a result of marine sediments or where water has come into contact with minerals. Most mineral springs produce cold water, but some are thermal (hot). The taste of mineral water in some areas is so undesirable in flavor that many choose to haul or buy their drinking water.

Hot Springs, Arkansas, for instance, features a thermal spring and has a long history of popularity; reportedly, Spanish conquistador Hernando de Soto used the water as early as 1542. The first bathhouses were in operation by 1830—and, two years later, President Andrew Jackson designated the hot spring as a national preserve—the nation's first. Hot Springs had seven bathhouses by the mid-1850s and was visited by Sam Houston, who was president of the Lone Star Republic (Texas).

The town of Eureka Springs in northwest Arkansas is also well-known for its mineral water. After the discovery of Eureka Springs' Basin Spring by Judge L.B. Saunders, he built a small house there in 1879. Before long, many others came and upon testing the "water that healed" exclaimed: "Eureka!"—which means "I have found it!" This is how the town came to receive its colorful name. Eureka Springs would come to be known as the "City of Healing Waters."

Eureka Springs grew by leaps and bounds and cooper shops built barrels and kegs in order to ship the "magic water" to destinations scattered all-over-the-world. In an 1881 article *Future Outlook For Eureka Springs* it reported that "Wealth, capital and enterprise are rapidly flowing in from all quarters, and large, handsome, substantial hotels, homes and business houses are rapidly taking the place of the ridiculous little box shanties which were hurriedly thrown together to meet the impatient demands for shelter. Hotels, boarding houses and every available habitation are full to overflowing; tents are springing up in all directions." It became a

Mills, Resorts, and Spas

health resort and prospered until the coming of modern medicine, when faith in natural cures declined.

In Cedar County, Missouri, the town of El Dorado Springs owes its existence to its famous mineral spring. Before this, however, Osage Indians and early settlers frequented the spring. By 1881, Nathanial H. and Waldo P. Cruce had designated the spring and 10-acres of land in the heart of El Dorado Springs to be the El Dorado Springs Public Park. Hundreds of invalids came with the hope and faith of being miraculously cured of their disabilities. In 1887 there were thirteen bottlers shipping the water all over the country; soda pop and ginger ale was also made from the mineral water. Late in the 1880s the railroad arrived which brought many tourists that prompted the need for more lodging, bathhouses, and merchants in the growing Ozarks spa town. (Also in Cedar County not far from El Dorado Springs is Jerico Springs, which is known as the "Fountain of Youth.")

Nearby in St. Clair County another well-known hamlet called Monegaw Springs enjoys a rich and colorful history because of its mineral spring. It is said that the name Monegaw, which reportedly means "owner of much money," came from an Osage Indian chief that, as legend has it, found some hidden Spanish silver in the area. Monegaw Springs was also a haunt and hideout for outlaws like the Younger gang—John Younger was shot and killed in a shoot-out with Pinkerton agents near there. The first settlers to arrive in the area was the Appleton family in 1834. By 1852, a large three-and-one-half story log hotel was constructed that overlooked the spring; the hotel burned in 1926.

Located a few miles east of Cassville, Missouri, in Barry County, seekers of mineral waters in the 1880s could find Panacea (later called Mineral Springs); a place that promoters claimed could cure rheumatism, kidney disease, and other things. They could ride the train to the Exeter Depot and then travel overland on a stagecoach to the spring. The short-line from Exeter to Cassville, which was a little more than 5 miles in distance and known as the Cassville and Western Railway, was not, however, celebrated until July 4, 1896. In an advertisement in the Cassville *Republican*, June 18, 1896, it shared the jubilance of its upcoming grand opening:

MONUMENTAL TALES FROM THE OZARKS

"The Cassville and Western Railway into Cassville is a cause for rejoicing and a matter of great moment. The management enters heartily into the celebration and all old settlers of the county from whatsoever portion they may come from will be given a free ride from Cassville to Exeter and return and special excursion rates will be given to all for the day both on the C&W and Frisco roads." Barry County's Mineral Springs grew and had several bathhouses, hotels, a post office, various stores, and other things—its demise came early in the 1960s.

There were many other resorts and spas that sprang up because of the abundance of Ozarks water, such as: Ponce de Leon, Reno, White Sulphur Springs, Sulphur Springs, Elk Springs, Aurora Springs, Zodiac Springs, Lithium, Radium, Excelsior Springs, Siloam Springs, and many others scattered across the Ozarks region and beyond.

The value and use of water is a precious resource for the future, and a look back into the past is proof enough of this fact. Throughout the Ozarks there still remain many places, relics, and ruins that oftentimes stir up curiosity and prompt further research and study about those old mills, resorts, and spas.

Bibliography

Alley Spring and Mill Historic Site
Bullard, Loring, *Healing Waters: Missouri's Historic Mineral Springs and Spas*, 2004.
Carter, Thad H., *Tracking the Past*, Litho Printers and Bindery, Cassville, Missouri, 2007.
Cassville *Republican*, June 18, 1896.
Future Outlook For Eureka Springs, Eureka Springs Carnegie Public Library, 1881.
Historic Marker and Signage, Eminence, Missouri.
Larkin, David, *Mill: The History and Future of Naturally Powered Buildings*, Universe Publishing, New York City, New York, 2000.
Mahnkey, Douglas, *Hill and Holler Stories*, College of the Ozarks Press, 1975.

Civil War monument at the National Cemetery No. 2 at Baxter Springs, Kansas.

Road to the Baxter Springs Massacre

Much of what transpired between Kansas and Missouri prior to the outbreak of the American Civil War, commonly called the Border War, prompted many citizens of these two states to side with either the North or the South. Before long, Civil War military actions further divided the states and many more made decisions about their loyalties—and some were forced to. Citizens began to cry out for justice and intervention; and neither side was willing to wait for the vengeance and judgment of God. Throughout those turbulent years, however, there would be plenty of revenge and atrocity to go around which would forever taint and stain American history and leave its audience continuing to ponder and evaluate its bloody execution.

The issue over the institution of slavery was reported to have enraged abolitionists from Kansas, who not only made raids into western Missouri to free them, but their trespassing also provided them a unique opportunity of earthly gain to plunder and loot their neighbors. John McCorkle, a scout who rode with the infamous, pro-Southern guerrilla William Clarke Quantrill, told about such raids carried out by Kansas Redlegs and their leaders like James H. Lane, Charles R. Jennison, and James Montgomery, and said that certain raiders would "forcibly take slaves into Kansas and hide them and when the Missouri owners would offer rewards for them, they would return the slaves, secure the reward, take several horses and cattle with them and return to Kansas, and, in a few weeks, return, steal the negroes again and collect another reward."

The Redlegs (so named for the red Moroccan leggings they wore) and their chief leaders so outraged Missourians that thousands would eventually offer their service to the Southern cause and to guerrilla forces—even Union supporters. In the long run, the work of men like Lane, Jennison, Montgomery, and others did little to abolish the sin of slavery or muster support for the Union. To make matters worse, the Federals had disarmed Missouri residents but did not unarm Kansans. A call for help went out to Washington from both sides but it fell, for the most part, on deaf ears.

On September 22, 1861, Federals from Kansas descended upon Osceola, Missouri, and according to Brigadier General James H. Lane he felt "compelled" to "shell out" the town's enemy inhabitants. As a result, Osceola was "burned to ashes, with an immense amount of stores of all descriptions." General Lane reported that about 20 were killed or wounded, but he said "we lost none...."

About the Missouri outrages, in the *Official Records of the Union and Confederate Armies* even Union Major General H.W. Halleck, reporting to the Secretary of War Edwin M. Stanton on March 25, 1862, wrote: "...in some cases horrible outrages have been committed by...The enemy's guerrilla bands...Kansas jayhawkers, or robbers, who were organized under the auspices of Senator [James H.] Lane. They wear the uniform of and it is believed receive pay from the United States. Their principle occupation for the last six months seems to have been the stealing of Negroes, the robbing of houses, and the burning of barns, grain, and forage. The evidence of their crimes is unquestionable. They have not heretofore been under my orders. I will now keep them out of Missouri or have them shot...."

Further fuel for the fire was undoubtedly created after Union Brigadier General Thomas Ewing ordered the arrest of seventeen young women who were charged with helping Quantrill and his men. Three of the girls, Josephine, Mary, and Jenny, were sisters of the infamous "Bloody" Bill Anderson, and some of the rest were friends, relatives, or sweethearts of Quantrill's men. The girls were imprisoned in an old rickety, abandoned structure at 1409 Grand

Avenue in Kansas City, Missouri. The makeshift jailhouse collapsed on August 13, 1863, however, and several of the young girls were killed, including Josephine Anderson and Charity Kerr who was a cousin of Cole, Jim, Bob, and John Younger. Mary Anderson was left crippled for life.

At daybreak on August 21, 1863, just eight days after the building collapsed on the seventeen imprisoned girls under Federal care, Quantrill, along with Bloody Bill Anderson, George Todd, William Gregg, Bill Gaw, Allen Parmer, Dick Maddox, Peyton Long, Dave Pool, Frank James, Cole Younger, and others rode into unsuspecting Lawrence, Kansas (the hometown of Lane and Jennison) on a mission of unspeakable terror and violence.

Author William Elsey Connelley who wrote *Quantrill and the Border Wars*, recounted the unholy massacre: "Demoniac yells rose above the crackling of pistol-shots...Victims were sought in homes, in shops, about the streets, in gardens, ravines, and fields of growing corn. Terror was carried to every heart...Fires were kindled in dwellings and shops and flames leaped and raced through all the streets and ways, consuming sometimes the living—often the dead. Shrieks of distress and cries of despair could be heard above the uproar and tumult raging in the city. Hell was loosed and the pent wrath and mad fury nursed for years by border-ruffians against Lawrence ran bloody riot in the pandemonium of that awful day."

By the time Quantrill's sacking of Lawrence had ended, though the exact number will never be known, about one hundred and fifty souls were killed in the history-making Lawrence Massacre. The town was in ruins and the streets were littered with lifeless bodies, and "piercing screams rose on the smoke-laden air...Women moaned piteously and wrung their hands in despair as they went from corpse to corpse peering into death-white faces in search of loved ones now missing."

Only four days later on August 25, 1863, with a nation outraged over this atrocity, Union Brig. Gen. Thomas Ewing retaliated and issued Military Order Number 11, one of the most controversial Orders of the American Civil War that left about 20,000 Missourians fleeing their homeland on a mass exodus; Order No. 11 forced the evacuation of Cass, Bates, Jackson, and part of Vernon counties in Missouri along the border with Kansas. About this, Connelley wrote: "The enforcement of Order No. 11 left almost nothing in the country upon which they could subsist. The Federal forces harried them day and night. The pursuit was grim, merciless, relentless, and many of them were killed."

A very vehement American who opposed General Order No. 11 was George Caleb Bingham, a well-known painter, soldier, and statesman from Missouri. Bingham kept a home in Arrow Rock, Mo., and is best known for his artwork, especially his painting depicting a scene of Order No. 11. In *Battles and Biographies of Missourians* by W.L. Webb, it quotes Bingham who wrote on February 22, 1877, about the difficulties Order No. 11 caused to Missouri's affected counties, saying that it was "...utterly desolated—its inhabitants driven from their homes, their dwellings committed to the flames, and their farms laid waste....

"Bare-footed and bare-headed women and children, stripped of every article of clothing except a scant covering for their bodies, were exposed to the heat of an August sun and compelled to struggle through the dust on foot....

"It is well-known that men were shot down in the very act of obeying the order, and their wagons and effects seized by their murderers. Large trains of wagons, extending over the prairies for miles in length, and moving Kansasward, were freighted with every description of household furniture and wearing apparel belonging to the exiled inhabitants. Dense columns of smoke arising in every direction marked the conflagrations of dwellings, many of the evidences of which are yet to be seen in the remains of seared and blackened chimneys, standing as melancholy monuments of a ruthless military despotism which spared neither age, sex, character, nor condition." The Missouri counties of Jackson, Cass, Bates, and Vernon became known as the "Burnt District."

A little over a month later on October 6, 1863, Quantrill and his bloodthirsty band of raiders, en route to Texas for the winter, learned of the newly constructed fort at Baxter Springs, Kansas. John McCorkle recalled that: "We all then rushed up the creek and to our utter surprise, we found a fort at Baxter Springs. None of us had ever heard that there was a fort there with a command of troops stationed in it."

The post was first called Fort Baxter and commanded by Lieutenant John Crites. The garrison was made up of the 3rd Wisconsin Cavalry, Company D, and the 2nd Kansas Colored Infantry under Lieutenant R.E. Cook. By October 5, however, Lieut. Crites who had been summoned to nearby Fort Scott was replaced by Lieutenant James B. Pond and the 3rd Wisconsin Cavalry, Company C, along with a 12-pound mountain howitzer artillery piece. The post was then officially designated to be Fort Blair, in honor of Lieutenant Colonel Charles W. Blair.

Baxter Springs, located on the "Fort Scott-Fort Gibson Military Road" (also known as the "Texas Road" or the "Immigrant Road to Texas"), a supply-line between the two posts during the Civil War, was described by Wiley Britton in *The Civil War on the Border* in this way: "From the early days in the war, Baxter Springs had been a noted camping ground for the Federal forces operating in Southern Kansas and the Indian Territory [Oklahoma]. It was a beautiful site for a camping ground, and was convenient to wood and water."

A large spring used by early settlers, explorers, and Native Americans flowed near the site of Fort Blair. However, because of area mining the spring has since dried up.

The fort, that Quantrill and his men were amazed to discover, was described in Connelley's book as consisting of "some log cabins with a total frontage of about a hundred feet, facing east— toward Spring river. These constituted the 'fort.' Back of the fort, and of the same width, was a large space enclosed by embankments of earth thrown up against logs and about four feet high. The west wall of the enclosure had been torn out the day before the attack by order of Lieutenant Pond, who found the camp too small for all the troops…The fort was half a mile west of Spring river."

Seizing the opportunity for some guerrilla warfare, Confederate Colonel Quantrill decided to make an attack on the unprepared Federals at Fort Blair. With about sixty of Lieut. Pond's men out foraging the countryside, there was only about "twenty-five white soldiers and seventy colored troops" left to defend the post.

It was about noon when the bloody foray began. From within the log breastworks came a rapid fire from the Federal troops while

Lieut. Pond manned the 12-pound gun, which eventually forced Quantrill's guerrillas and irregulars in a cloud of black powder smoke and screaming cannonballs to retreat to safety beyond their death-dealing range. The rapid cannonading of Lieut. Pond's big gun must have impressed John McCorkle who later said that "Quantrill turned to me and told me to get the boys away from the fort and to form in line. Just as I had succeeded, the Federals fired from the fort with their two cannon, one of the balls literally decapitating Dave Woods."—remember, Lieut. Pond only had one artillery piece. According to Lieut. Pond (at this point in the battle), there were eight killed and several wounded.

Meanwhile, on the Military Road, Union Major General James G. Blunt had left Fort Scott a couple of days before on his way to Fort Smith, Arkansas, with about 125 men from the 3rd Wisconsin Cavalry under Lieutenant J.G. Cavert, the 14th Kansas Cavalry commanded by Lieutenant R.H. Pierce, and his brigade band, clerks, and orderlies; they were nearing the fort unaware of Quantrill's presence. Wiley Britton reported that "his escort came up, and while waiting a few moments for his wagons to close up, his attention was called to about 150 mounted men, some three hundred yards to his left, forming in line and advancing from the timber on Spring River....

"General Blunt and his Assistant Adjutant General, Major Curtis, endeavored to rally the men; but it was impossible to rally them against greatly superior numbers in an open prairie, and the bandits closed in upon them, and in the pursuit of two or three miles, shot down and killed all the men overtaken, wounded, or captured, except about a dozen who feigned death after they were terribly wounded."

The force that Gen. Blunt had encountered was none other than Quantrill who had discovered the Federal train, ambulance, and buggies on the prairie leading to the fort. John McCorkle recounted how they "went at them in our accustomed manner, yelling and shooting...."

Gen. Blunt lost about ninety percent of his military escort but was able to somehow escape through the enemy ranks and rally his surviving troops to reach Baxter Springs and Fort Blair. It didn't go as well for his men left on the battleground; some of their bodies were piled in and under a wagon and set ablaze. When they were discovered later on by their fellow comrades, it wasn't a pretty sight; they were "horribly burned and disfigured."

Gen. Blunt reported that there was seventy-nine killed and several unaccounted for as a result of the attack. Blunt also reported that Col. Quantrill had about 600 men during the fight; however, Quantrill reported a different count of 250 men.

The battlefield covered several miles and the following day was spent burying the victims of the massacre. Over the years many Civil War artifacts have been found in the area; and even the remains of two bodies were once unearthed by a farmer's plow—they were buried at the National Cemetery No. 2 in Baxter Springs along with others who died in the attack.

The many actions and events that led to the Baxter Springs Massacre, one of only a few Civil War battles that occurred in Kansas, will forever be a source of study and debate. But for whatever the reason or cause, it should at least be agreed upon that it is a road or path best not traveled or taken—ever again.

Bibliography

Barton, O. S., *Three Years with Quantrill*, Armstrong Herald Printing, 1914.

Britton, Wiley, *The Civil War on the Border*, G.P. Putnam's Sons, The Knickerbocker Press, 1899.

Connelley, William Elsey, *Quantrill and the Border Wars*, Cedar Rapids, Iowa, The Torch Press, 1910.

Official Records of the Union and Confederate Armies, Washington: Government Printing Office, 1881.

Webb, W. L., *Battles and Biographies of Missourians* or *The Civil War Period of Our State*, Hudson-Kimberly Publishing Company, Kansas City, Missouri, 1900.

Blast fragments from the explosion at Noel, Missouri, on display at Har-Ber Village in Grove, Oklahoma.

Memorable Disasters

The Ozarks has endured a number of devastating disasters that brought destruction and death. Some of the stories have been recorded in newspapers, magazines, and books; and some are still fresh in the minds of those who remember them. One such memorable event occurred on a hot summer day in Jasper County, Missouri, when residents were suddenly rocked to their senses by a series of tremendous explosions and shock waves. Until the facts were known, many thought that blast was a nuclear detonation, a commercial airline crash, or some sort of attack. The unforgettable tragedy, however, that had seismographs busy as far away as Denver, Colorado, briefly brought this peaceful Ozarks community into the world's spotlight.

It was early afternoon, July 14, 1966, at the Hercules Powder Company a few miles west of Carthage, Mo., when a truck-fire in a storage area of high explosives started a chain of blasts in the plant complex. The craters that were formed, by one account, was compared to the potted lunar surface. A massive mushroom cloud rose high into the air as about 70 percent of the Hercules Powder Company was blown to smithereens. The smoke from the burning plant went more than 5,000 feet into the air above the 1,200-acre "Hercules" site.

Debris from the magazine areas were found two miles away and extensive damage was caused to homes and businesses over a five-mile radius. Car windshields were shattered and their sides were caved-in by the force of the blast. Hundreds of rural homes and buildings in the Hercules area were damaged and their windows broken or blown out.

Some of the worst damage was found to have occurred at what was known as "Powertown," a small community that sprang up near Hercules where many of the employees and their families lived. It was reported that at least 40 of the homes in Powdertown were destroyed or in bad condition, as a result.

Minor damage was caused in nearby Webb City and Carterville, but Carthage received the worst of it—the Joplin *Globe* listed about 28 downtown businesses that were affected. The beautiful historic square was roped off because of the massive amount of debris that littered the streets.

There was rapid on-the-spot response from about sixteen area fire departments, but because of concerns that the main powder magazine could still explode in the blast zone, they were kept back for a time from entering the Hercules complex. While all of this was taking place, local authorities were busy evacuating residents in a four-mile radius of ground zero. There was ongoing action by the Civil Defense, Red Cross, Salvation Army, Sheriff's Department, and others who gave their undivided attention. The Missouri Army National Guard were called in to address the problems that arose concerning looting in the area; and also to assist in rescue, communications, and cleanup.

About 36 victims of the monumental event were treated at Carthage's McCune-Brooks Hospital, and several others underwent ongoing hospital care. There was one death as a result of the explosions, Maurice A. Crowell, a shipping clerk who worked at Hercules Powder Company. It was reported by the sheriff that Crowell was found wearing only his shoes—the blast had blown off all of his clothes!

Fires raged for some time after the event, but eventually things returned to normal. The overwhelming participation and contributions made by area agencies and unsung heroes, undoubtedly, saved the public from further disaster, injury, and loss of life.

Another incident to hit the Ozarks occurred in Noel, Missouri. Known for its unique bluffs and overhanging cliffs, refreshing

Memorable Disasters

rivers, and its Christmas-time postage mark Noel made newspaper headlines when the community was suddenly rocked by a devastating explosion—much like the one that happened at the Hercules Powder Company in Carthage. At a time when most papers were covering stories about President Richard Nixon, the Vietnam War, POWs, and Mariner 7 streaking across the polar cap of the "Red Plant" Mars, many front pages in the peaceful Ozarks region ran the breaking news story of a disastrous catastrophe that struck the small southwestern Missouri town of Noel in the wee hours of a summer morning.

It was August 3, 1969, at 3:55 a.m., when a 115-car train No. 77, traveling on the Kansas City Southern railway, was making its way southbound through Noel en route from Kansas City, Mo., to Shreveport, Louisiana, when an observant brakeman noticed a fire burning on a flatbed car. The train car was loaded with ammonium perchlorate, which was consigned to the Department of Defense. As crewmen were in the process of uncoupling this portion of the train, in order to get the blazing car out of town, the fire ignited the adjacent car loaded with dehydrated alfalfa; it was about one block south of the Kansas City Southern depot. The blast that followed would suddenly startle and awaken scores of sleeping citizens, who would later learn what had happened. They would soon be amazed to discover that a huge crater was ripped out of the track roadbed about 6-feet deep, 60-feet long, and 40-feet wide; completely obliterating five other train cars in the process.

The explosion was heard as far away as Anderson, Mo. to the north and, Rogers, Arkansas to the south. The massive shockwaves from the blast brought down roofs and walls, shattered windows, and stripped off tree leaves over a five block area. It was reported that 31 residential homes were ruined beyond repair, 58 were badly damaged, and 55 more were moderately affected. Most of the windows in the downtown area were blown out by the tremendous force, leaving glass and debris to litter the streets and sidewalks. It was said that 58 businesses were also damaged or destroyed because of the blast.

Automobiles were also affected in the blast zone, with broken and shattered windshields and their tops and sides cave-in by the shockwave. Various sized parts and fragments of the demolished railroad cars were catapulted blocks away, causing damage and severing power-lines which cut off service to most of the town.

An 800-pound train wheel was reported to have been propelled through the air with such velocity that it crashed through the roof of one house, into a bedroom, through two partitions into the living room and, finally, the massive projectile came to rest against the outside wall of the house—this was more than two blocks from the site of the explosion.

Within minutes of the awful catastrophe, area fire departments, police, and rescue units responded from four states. In Missouri they came from Neosho, Diamond, Granby, Pineville, Southwest City, Carl Junction, Webb City, Joplin, Monett, Carthage, and Aurora; participating from Kansas was Galena, Pittsburg, and Baxter Springs; from Arkansas, Fayetteville, Bentonville, Rogers, Sulphur Springs, Gravette, and Decatur; and from Oklahoma, Miami, and Jay answered the call. The damaged area was sealed off by the National Guard of Neosho, Anderson, and Carthage—only residents and workmen were allowed in the zone.

As a result of the disaster only one person was killed, a victim of a piece of flying debris. About 60 other persons were injured and were taken to area hospitals in Arkansas, Missouri, and Oklahoma. Those at the scene thought that there could have been more injured if the incident would have happened when people were up and going about their daily routines.

Still yet another example of trial and tribulation caused by disaster is the threat of severe weather and the all-to-familiar signs—dark, ominous clouds, dropping temperatures, heavy rain, hail, and strong winds. All too often nature's fury can suddenly and with scant warning deliver a devastating blow. This was the case in Barry County, Missouri, on April 18, 1880, when angry clouds formed into history-making funnels.

The deadly event was recorded in *Goodspeed's History of Barry County*. The twisters "...swept through the county in two parts or sections, creating more havoc in a few minutes than did the troops of the Union and Confederate Governments in four years." The death-hungry tornadoes formed about 4 p.m. and "chased each other

Memorable Disasters

to and fro over the Shoal Creek Valley; a little later they moved forward rapidly and formed...seven miles northwest of Cassville."

Witnesses in Barry County reported that "The wind was so high at every point, and its speed so swift, few could realize that any section of Southwest Missouri suffered from the storm more than that particular section in which they resided, until the news of destruction was brought to Cassville, and spread thence to every settlement."

The tornadoes didn't stop with Barry County, they continued meandering on to the northeast and caused more havoc in Christian, Greene, and Webster counties; other places were also in the path. Cassville residents would soon learn about the ninety-two souls that perished in the Ozarks town of Marshfield as a result of the twisters; they would also learn that the "forces combined to destroy that town" of about 150 homes and many businesses.

The death toll in Barry County, however, despite the overall destruction, was light—a 4-year-old child was killed by a chimney collapse and a few others died of their injuries. Many, though, were seriously hurt; some citizens were crippled, and there were reports of a nearly severed leg, hurt ankle, crushed shoulder, broken bones, and other things.

One family was saved by getting "under a ledge of rock on the creek bank" while another family "took refuge in a well, and escaped being carried away with their dwellings." There were reports of seeing the "house and barns flying with the clouds" and "property blown down or carried off by the terrific house-robber..." or "the destroyer carrying off their homes and furniture."

There were animals and livestock killed in the area—horses and hogs, as well as many trees damaged and uprooted. There were schools damaged or destroyed, and mills suffering the same fate. The nearby hamlet of McDowell was completely swept away during the unforgiving event. Goodspeed summed it up by saying that: "Other evidences of destruction marked the path of this terrible storm."

Bibliography

Goodspeed's History of Barry County, Goodspeed Publishing Company, 1888.

Jackson, Rex T., *Barry County's Perfect Storm*, Vol. 5, No. 1, 2008, The Ozarks Reader Magazine, Neosho, Missouri; *Jasper County's Herculean Blast*, Vol. 3, No. 2, 2006, The Ozarks Reader Magazine, Neosho, Missouri; *Noel's Train Car Explosion of 1969*, Vol. 1, 2004, The Ozarks Reader Magazine, Neosho, Missouri.

Joplin *Globe*, July 15, 1966.

Joplin *Globe*, August 4, 5, 1969.

VanGilder, Marvin L., *Jasper County: The First Two Hundred Years*, 1995.

Warning sign near the site of the Hercules Power Company in Jasper County, Missouri.

Harvey and Bernice Jones at the entrance to
Har-Ber Village, Grove, Oklahoma.

Harvey and Bernice Jones' Har-Ber Village

The Ozarks has, for a number of years, benefited from the openhanded generosity of two individuals, Harvey and Bernice Jones who created Har-Ber Village located in Grove, Oklahoma—a place where multitudes have visited. One of the regions best kept secrets, it hosts people from near and far who wander its spacious, scenic grounds overlooking the Grand Lake of the Cherokees on a self-guided tour of America's past—courtesy of the Jones'.

It all started in 1918 when Harvey and Bernice Jones decided to create a business to transport needed goods between Springdale, Rogers, and Fayetteville, Arkansas. At first, Harvey used a mule-team and wagon to make deliveries, but by 1919 he had upgraded to a truck and expanded his business to include Ft. Smith, Ark., and Joplin and Springfield, Missouri. By 1933 the Springdale Transportation Company, as it was called, became the Jones Truck Lines, Inc. It would become the largest privately-owned trucking firm in the United States, serving 15 states and employing about 1,500 people; however, Harvey eventually sold the business in 1980.

Both Harvey and Bernice, who were married for 51 years, were active in the community and were generous with their time and money. Harvey served as Chairman of the Springdale Memorial Hospital Board, President of the School Board, President of the Chamber of Commerce, and Chairman of the Board of the First National Bank of Springdale, among other things.

MONUMENTAL TALES FROM THE OZARKS

Har-Ber Village began by accident when Harvey decided to build a little church for Bernice on the banks of a rolling Ozarks wooded acreage they bought in 1944. After the Church, which could be seen from "Grand Lake," began to attract curious souls ashore who were boating on the lake, the Jones' were encouraged to add more to what eventually became an "antique village" of over 100 log cabins and other buildings.

Bernice named the Village, that all started with the little Church, Har-Ber, after the first three letters of their first names. A memorial stone at the base of the Village Bell Tower sums up the purpose of the Jones' unique monumental contribution, which reads: "A sincere effort to preserve for future generations the way of life as experienced by our forefathers who carved out of the wilderness this wonderful country we know and enjoy today."

Within Har-Ber Village, besides the Church which was built using pre-Civil War fireplace bricks salvaged from the old Van Winkle home of War Eagle, Ark., there is a one-room Schoolhouse moved from the Goshen, Ark., area; the Bank woodworking relocated from Carterville, Mo.; and the Drug Store soda fountain from Pettigrew, Ark. Visitors can also discover a Courthouse, Hanging Gallows, Jail, Indian Museum, Post Office, Stagecoach Inn, Waterwheel, Covered Wagon, General Mercantile, Dentist's Office, Barber Shop, Mayor's House, Doll and Glass House, Hillbilly House, and the Furniture House; as well as displays of pottery, glass, military items, musical instruments, farm machinery, guns, and just about anything from our nation's past.

Harvey Jones died in 1989, and Bernice Jones who shared equally in all of Harvey's activities continued the work they had done together as a team. Many organizations, such as libraries, museums, colleges, and universities benefited from Bernice's ongoing generosity. She became the first woman to serve on the Board of Directors for the Springdale Memorial Hospital; and would support it the rest of her life. Bernice also helped to establish a school of nursing and was a Chairperson of the Harvey and Bernice Jones Eye Institute Advisory Board at the University of Arkansas in Little Rock for Medical Science. Before Bernice died, however, she received many well-deserved awards and recognitions for her life's work.

The Jones' trucking success, which more or less started because of a lingering northwest Arkansas railroad strike, went on to become a highway to the many generous gifts they left behind. Even though Har-Ber Village became a great collection of American and Ozarks past, it also became a place where many can come to know, to some degree, Harvey and Bernice Jones.

Bibliography

Har-Ber Village, Grove, Oklahoma.
Jackson, Rex T., *Har-Ber Village: The Many Gifts of Harvey and Bernice Jones*, Vol. 5, No. 2, 2008, The Ozarks Reader Magazine, Neosho, Missouri.

Ha Ha Tonka ruins at the Ha Ha Tonka State Park near Camdenton, Missouri.

Ha Ha Tonka: R.M. Snyder's Dream Castle Ruins

Out of place in the Ozarks region not far from Camdenton, Missouri, is a massive ruins of monumental proportions, a structure more reminiscent of a European castle but unexpected in its placement. The castles that are scattered throughout Europe's countryside, however, were made for medieval lords and monarchs, and the word castle, *castellum*, means "a fortified place"—made to last.

Many castles were built high upon impregnable perches; oftentimes, overlooking a river with a commanding view of the surrounding landscape. In such a well-situated location, the imposing house was more impervious to intrusion or invasion. The popularity and usefulness of the castles eventually, around 1500, became less necessary after the advent of gunpowder projectiles. Remaining castles then fell into disrepair or were used primarily for mansions.

High on a bluff with a commanding presence overlooking Lake of the Ozarks is the castle ruins of R.M. Snyder—now known as Ha Ha Tonka State Park. The Ha Ha Tonka State Park is located in Camden County and was designated as a state park in 1978. The Park is a wonderland of natural beauty which features "karst" topography (ancient underground collapsed caverns, caves, springs, and natural bridges); savannas (areas that are part prairie and part timber); 15 miles of trails; a Visitor Center; and serving as the centerpiece of the Park is the castle ruin that sets 250-feet above

MONUMENTAL TALES FROM THE OZARKS

Lake of the Ozarks.

It all started when Robert McClure Snyder, a highly successful businessman from Kansas City, Missouri, visited the area in 1903. Snyder liked what he saw and went on to purchase 5,000-arces of land for his planned dream home and country retreat. His grand, cliff-side manor ideas, however, went far beyond ordinary mindset. Snyder began work on his European-Renaissance-style three-and-one-half-story, gray limestone, twenty-eight-room manse in 1905. The selected building site of the massive structure was on a summit known as "Deer Leap Hill" above Ha Ha Tonka Spring. The work ended abruptly, though, when Snyder was killed in a car accident in October 1906—one of Missouri's first recorded automobile fatalities.

Before long, Snyder's sons continued their father's grandiose dream working intermittently until 1922. The completed cost of the castle-manse was more than $300,000—a large sum at the time. They encountered several adversities during the process, selling business interests, the Depression, and a long legal battle before the Missouri Supreme Court to halt the creation of Bagnell Dam which was eventually constructed near the town of Lake Ozark and just north of Osage Beach. The dam was built across the Osage River to form Lake of the Ozarks in order to produce hydroelectric power; Lake of the Ozarks is the largest lake in Missouri and boasts 1,400 miles of shoreline. The Snyder family believed that the waters of Lake of the Ozarks would cause a great deal of flood damage to their sizeable property. The financial burden of these problems forced them to lease the property and castle out to be used as a hotel. As a result, in 1942 chimney sparks ignited the roof and fire gutted the entire structure; the nearby stables and carriage house were also lost to flames—and, to finish the tragedy, the 80-foot water tower that supplied the mansion with gravity-flow water was burned and gutted by vandals in 1976.

In Robert McClure Snyder's obituary in the Kansas City *Journal*, October 29, 1906, it offered a bit of insight into his character, saying that he was the kind of man that "...understood big things and made them win by keeping up the fight when other men might have been ready to give up."

Ha Ha Tonka: R.M. Snyder's Dream Castle Ruins

The castle ruins that seems unlikely to the Ozarks can offer a look back into a turn-of-the-century (1900) dream that still continues to command the summit at Ha Ha Tonka. The European-style retreat still whispers human inspiration and monumental accomplishment, even in its ruined state.

Bibliography

Funk & Wagnalls New Encyclopedia, Funk & Wagnalls, Inc., New York, 1979.

Ha Ha Tonka State Park, Camdenton, Missouri.

Kansas City *Journal*, October 29, 1906.

Carthage Carnegie Public Library in Carthage, Missouri.

Andrew Carnegie: Libraries of Generosity

In 1890 it was reported that more than half of the nation's wealth was owned by 1 percent of the population. And even earlier than that in 1873, a congressional inquiry into the matter reported that the nation was "fast becoming filled with gigantic corporations wielding and controlling immense aggregations of money and thereby commanding great influence and power."

Some well-to-do Americans believed in "social Darwinism"— the strong survive and the weak die out. They argued that citizens need only to work hard to attain wealth and money, and if it didn't happen, there must be a flaw in their character.

There was at least one American, Andrew Carnegie who attempted to refute such doctrine, to some degree. Carnegie founded the Carnegie Steel Company (later known as U.S. Steel) and amassed a fortune in the steel industry. By 1900, Carnegie was supplying one-quarter of the nation's hunger for steel. Tycoon Carnegie believed, contrary to the social Darwinism group, that it was best to set an example and give back accumulated wealth to communities where struggling citizens lived. He was especially a firm believer in public libraries as a means of helping to self-educate people, as well as providing cultural institutions and schools across the nation.

In 1889, Andrew Carnegie wrote the *Gospel of Wealth* which was published in the *North American Review*, and in it he said that millionaires were only a "mere trustee and agent for his poorer brethren, bringing to their service his superior wisdom, experience, and ability to administer, doing for them better than they could or would do for themselves." Carnegie put forth the notion that life comes in two parts: first, to acquire wealth; and second, to give it away.

Carnegie was true-to-his-word and for one of his many contributions as a philanthropist he helped to construct more than 2,000 libraries all over the world; some of them in the Ozarks region. Every community dreams of and benefits from a public library. Those that are fortunate enough to have access to such a facility can research important local, American, and world history; stay on top of current events and become knowledgeable about local, state, national, and international topics; trace genealogy; be entertained, enlightened, and a host of other worthwhile things pertinent to any thriving, civilized culture.

One such Ozarks library that owes a great deal to Andrew Carnegie is the Carthage Public Library in Carthage, Missouri. The Carthage community began to organize and establish a public library as early as 1870. Funds were raised and a library was opened in a small storefront located on the town's Main Street. However, at the turn-of-the-century in 1902, the Carnegie Foundation of New York provided a total of $25,000 to be paid in lumps of $5,000 as needed during construction of a new, more impressive library in Carthage. To receive the funds, Carthage citizens were required to pass a tax levy to support the library and find an acceptable location to build it—they did both!

According to a letter dated August 14, 1902, from R.A. Franks, president of the Home Trust Company of Hoboken, New Jersey, on behalf of the proposal, he enclosed a certificate and affidavit from the Carthage Library Board of Directors concerning a tract of land suitable for the library that was to be built "with the funds so cheerfully donated by the Honorable Andrew Carnegie."

The proposal describes the location as being "an ideal one fronting our beautiful Central Park which lies immediately across the street to the south, which is a tract of five acres covered with a natural growth of beautiful oak trees through and under which during the hot summer months the Library will have the benefit of

Andrew Carnegie: Libraries of Generosity

cool breezes that invariably come from the south and southwest over the prairies of Texas and the Indian Territory from the Gulf of Mexico. This site is in the heart of the city...."

The proposal being accepted the work on the Carthage Public Library began at 612 S. Garrison Avenue in 1903 using Carthage stone. Architect Frederick Gunn of Kansas City, Mo., built the library after a neoclassic style. It opened to the waiting public on February 2, 1905, with about 3,000 to 5,000 books; the first volume "checked-out" was *Ben Hur*; and Miss Elizabeth Wales was named as the first director of the library.

In 2003, however, Jasper County voters approved a sales tax increase to fund a renovation and addition to the Carthage Public Library which would double the space of the original Carnegie structure to 13,200 sq. ft. The new addition opened in May 2007, with a ribbon cutting on February 9, 2008. The architect for the new addition was Gould Evans, also of Kansas City, Mo.

Another beautiful Carnegie library was built in Eureka Springs, Arkansas. The town's location was described in an article *The Resort of the Ozarks* published in 1906, in this way: "A twelve hours' ride from either St. Louis, Kansas City, Dallas, Memphis, Oklahoma City or Little Rock will bring the traveler to the Ozark Range of Mountains. And on the summit of those mountains is the city of Eureka Springs...."

The historic Eureka Springs Carnegie Public Library is located at 194 Spring Street and began in 1910 and was completed by 1912. The Classical Revival limestone structure was built with $12,000 donated by Andrew Carnegie and the Carnegie Foundation of New York. The Eureka Springs Carnegie Public Library is part of the Carroll County and Madison County Library System of Arkansas. The library offers support and service for the community and for preschool, grade school, and high school students.

Still another Carnegie library was built in Webb City, Mo., in 1914 with funds from the Carnegie Foundation of New York. The Richardsonian Romanesque structure was constructed of native limestone boulders trimmed out in Carthage stone. Its doors and windows were enhanced by arches and stained glass and the interior was crafted in red oak woodworking.

MONUMENTAL TALES FROM THE OZARKS

In August 2002, however, voters approved a one-eighth-cent sales tax to cover a loan of $2,000,000 which would be paid off in about 20 years (along with additional funds from donations and other sources), to double the size of the original library from 9,800 sq. ft. to 18,600 sq. ft.; the new Webb City Carnegie Public Library was rededicated on April 10, 2005.

Carnegie's compassion and generosity has proved over the years to have benefited the public in many and various ways—still, the poor wait for more opportunity to "trickle-down" as the struggle between the ideas like those of Carnegie and those of social Darwinism continue to play out in America. There is no way to know how long the monumental contributions left by Andrew Carnegie will last, but his less avarice example should continue to stalk and pursue the human conscience and experience for as long as it is needed.

Bibliography

The American Journey: A History of the United States, Prentice Hall, Upper Saddle River, New Jersey, 1998.

The American Promise: A History of the United States, Bedford Books, Boston, 1998.

Carnegie, Andrew, *Gospel of Wealth*, North American Review, 1889.

Carthage Carnegie Public Library, Library Records, Carthage, Missouri.

Chronicle of America, Chronicle Publications, Mount Kisco, New York, 1988.

Eureka Springs Carnegie Public Library, Library Records, Eureka Springs, Arkansas.

The Resort of the Ozarks, (Pamphlet), Eureka Springs Carnegie Public Library, Eureka Springs, Arkansas, 1906.

The George Dimmitt Hospital building in Humansville, Missouri.

George Dimmitt Memorial Hospital

In early American times, medical care was, for the most part, miles away and transporting the sick and injured was accomplished by horse and buggy, wagon, or by other less modern means. The trails were rough and rugged and many perished en route. One small Ozark town in Polk County offered a monumental gesture of mercy when it brought lifesaving health care to the community; and honored one of its citizens in the process.

The first hospital in the United States, the Pennsylvania Hospital, was established in 1751 in Philadelphia, Pennsylvania, by the efforts of statesman Benjamin Franklin and a local doctor. During the 19th century many health facilities were created, mostly because of the advent of anesthesia and aseptic (infection-preventing) surgical techniques.

In Humansville, Missouri, the George Dimmitt Memorial Hospital was the brainchild of Mr. and Mrs. Charles E. Dimmitt. The facility was made not only to serve the much needed medical needs of the area, but to honor the tragic loss of their beloved son, George H. Dimmitt who was born in Humansville. The hospital was dedicated to the community on November 21, 1929.

According to the Humansville *Star Leader*, dated August 1, 1929, it reported that the north wing of the structure was originally the brick home of Mrs. Harriot Beason. The main building and south wing were constructed in such a way as to give "symmetry" to the whole facility, and the work was carried out by the Easley

Brothers Company of Aurora, Missouri.

The hospital had colonial front porches that graced the north and south wings, and inside there were two Terrazzo floored corridors that were eight feet wide and 70-feet long. The hospital rooms were given white maple flooring; while the operating rooms received white tile. The X-Ray room was equipped with the well-known "Victor X-Ray" machines; and the facility had a 6 x 10-foot "Otis Electric Elevator" installed.

The hospital was operated as a non-profit organization—billing charges were only enough to cover expenses. However, no expense was spared in equipping the facility with the best and latest lifesaving equipment of the times.

The George Dimmitt Memorial Hospital officially opened to the public on November 25, 1929, and served the Humansville community until 1973. Its closing was a result of increasing state regulations that strained its funds, which made it too difficult to continue operation. The one-time, lifesaving health care facility was eventually sold at public auction.

The Humansville hospital that the Dimmitt's named to honor their lost son, over-the-years, undoubtedly saved many lives. It is a testament to early medical facilities that delivered much care and mercy to Ozark citizens in need—a fitting memorial and tribute to George H. Dimmitt.

George Dimmitt Memorial Hospital

Bibliography

Funk & Wagnalls New Encyclopedia, Funk & Wagnalls, Inc., New York, 1979.
Humansville *Star Leader*, August 1, 1929.
Humansville Public Library

Historic monument at the old Spanish Fort in Lawrence County, Missouri.

Old Spanish Fort: Legend and Lore

The Ozarks region is no stranger to legends and folklore of the hunt for gold and silver. Wild tales have been handed down over the years about the conquest of riches by Spanish treasure hunters who came to the untamed Ozarks wilderness.

Silver has been coveted for coinage and jewelry since ancient times. The first known silver mining occurred in Asia Minor around 2500 B.C. The use of silver for minting coins can be traced to the latter part of the 8th century B.C. The United States' first national mint was created in 1792 in Philadelphia, Pennsylvania—America's capital at the time. The Bureau of the Mint, a branch of the United States Department of the Treasury was established in 1873.

The purest form of silver has most generally been found in Peru and Norway; however, silver is also a byproduct of the mining of lead, copper, and zinc ores. Small amounts of copper, gold, and other precious minerals are also obtained through the processing of the ore. Lead and zinc have been mined in abundance in the Ozark Mountains—and, for good reason, a number of legends have been told and passed down as a result.

On a hill overlooking and sandwiched between Honey Creek and Spring River in Lawrence County, Missouri, a prehistoric site known as the old "Spanish Fort" or "Fort Ancient" can be found; an old cemetery is also located there. Its remote location near the hamlet of Hobert a few miles southwest of Mt. Vernon, Mo., has left the historic landmark hidden and unknown to most.

Over the years a local legend has lingered that contends that the ancient fort was built by Spaniards who came to Missouri in search of gold and other precious metals. Hernando De Soto, a Spanish explorer, probably came the closest. It is believed that De Soto landed on the west coast of Florida in 1539 with about 1000 men, where they proceeded to explore Florida, the Carolina's, Alabama, Mississippi, Arkansas, Oklahoma, and northern Texas. The treasure hunt finally ended in the spring of 1542—empty handed. However, De Soto never returned to Spain after his explorations, he died of a fever and his men weighted his body and sank his remains in the Mississippi River.

A historic monument dedicated on October 16, 1930, at the fort's site by the Springfield University Club of Springfield, Mo., which, for the most part, robs the Spanish of any connection to the fort, reads: "Fort Ancient, believed to have been constructed by a group of eastward migrating mound builders, a band of Indians probably long antedating the Osages, on their way to what is now Ohio. These earthworks are a small replica of the great Fort Ancient in Ohio, where this prehistoric group reached its greatest culmination. This tribe probably had a village in the valley and used these fortifications for defense. First pioneers describe the walls as originally about five feet high and the moat two feet deep." The back of the marker reads: "Locally known as the old Spanish Fort."

Another historic marker in downtown Verona, Mo., states that the fort was "built by prehistoric tribes. Indians roamed the area, part of 1808 Osage cession, into the 1830's."

In *The Ozarks Region: Its History and Its People* by E.S. Allen, published in 1917, it describes the fort and says that it "was built in a circle and contained about 1 ½ acres. On the north and south, about 150 feet from the main fort, there were wings about 200 feet long...."

The grounds were eventually made into a cemetery by landowners Thomas and Ellon Allen; Ellon became the first interment to the cemetery. Many of the headstones are of people born in the 1700s and died in the late 1800s.

The fact that treasure hunting has long been reported in the Ozarks, and that the Spanish once roamed and explored a vast amount of America's wilderness, is indisputable. But whether or not

Old Spanish Fort: Legend and Lore

the Spaniards wandered as far north as Lawrence County, Missouri, remains a monumental tale of legend and lore which some still find appealing.

Bibliography

Allen, E.S., *The Ozarks Region: Its History and Its People*, Vol. 2, Interstate Historical Society, Springfield, Missouri, 1917.

Funk & Wagnalls New Encyclopedia, Funk & Wagnalls, Inc., New York, 1979.

Historic Marker, Verona, Missouri.

Historic Monument, Old Spanish Fort, Lawrence County, Missouri.

Smelting works near St. James, Missouri, about fifty miles west of Potosi.

Moses and Stephen Austin: Icons of Missouri and Texas

Opportunities in the West inspired many to face the unknown and chase their dreams of a better, more prosperous life. They made numerous sacrifices and endured many hardships in the process. In the wild open spaces beyond the Mississippi River lurked uncertain dangers, but also rich land and possibilities. These things stirred the minds of men like Daniel Boone and Moses Austin.

Moses Austin was born in Connecticut in October 1761. When Moses was 22-years-old he joined an import company that was expanding its interest in the mining industry, and by 1789 he had founded a branch office in Richmond, Virginia. Before long, he had become the owner of some lead mines in southwestern Virginia, which he worked with slave labor. After hearing about plentiful lead deposits in the Upper Louisiana Territory of present-day Missouri, he saddled up his horse in 1796 and headed out. While riding through Illinois, Austin became lost in a blinding snowstorm but eventually reached the Mississippi River and St. Louis. He pressed on with permission to explore the territory about 40 miles west of Ste. Genevieve. When he reached "Mine a Burton" (Potosi) he found it to be just as he had been told, rich in lead ore. In the hills around the site of Potosi were smelting furnaces and the evidence of hand-dug mining activity. The settlement was without people, however, as the miners probably traveled from Ste. Genevieve and surrounding places to work at the site. In a valley flowed a babbling brook of clear water and Austin could see grand opportunity there for a growing business and a prosperous Potosi community. It didn't take him long to hightail it back to Virginia to take care of business and tie up loose ends. Returning to Potosi, Austin floated down the Kanawha and Ohio Rivers and then finally working upriver on the Mississippi to reach Ste. Genevieve with his wife Maria, 5-year-old Stephen, little Emily and several others including slaves.

Before long, Austin had become wealthy in the lead mining business, opened his own store, and had investment in a bank in St. Louis. Potosi soon boasted a courthouse, post office, jailhouse, school, mills, homes and all the benefits of a thriving but slave-driven society (in some cases). In 1803, after the Louisiana Purchase, he was named presiding judge for the District of Ste. Genevieve. Following the Panic of 1819—runaway depreciation and wild speculation after the War of 1812, Austin lost his fortune and set his sights on a scheme to colonize Spanish Territory (Texas). The Panic of 1819 left many Mississippi River Valley settlers considering relocation.

Moses traveled west and applied for and received a land grant from the Spanish governor early in 1821 for 18,000 square miles of land within the territory of Texas for 300 American colonists. When Moses Austin returned to Missouri that same year with the good news, he became ill and died on June 10, 1821, and was buried in a vault at a cemetery just off the square in Potosi. Moses' son Stephen who grew up in Potosi, played with Indian children that came to their store and roamed the Ozarks hills and hollows, was left to carry on and finish what his father had started.

Stephen Fuller Austin was born in Wythe County, Virginia, and was sent back East from Potosi to get his education at Transylvania University. He served from 1814 to 1820 in Missouri's Territorial legislature. After the death of Moses he traveled to Texas and became the first *empresario* (land agent)—selling parcels to land-hungry frontiersmen; the land that his father had secured was located between the Colorado and Brazos Rivers. Part of the agreement with Mexico, however, was that they would all have to become Mexican citizens and Catholic—forced religion.

The first legal American colony grew rapidly and Stephen ruled over it with dictatorial-like powers using a land-grant system for newcomers, promoting industry, education and fending off hostile Indian attacks. In 1823, after Mexico had gained independence from Spain in late 1821, Austin traveled to Mexico City to reconfirm his land grant status with the new government for the Texas settlement. The colony had grown by leaps and bounds to a population of about 14,000 whites and about 400 slaves by 1825. However, the Texas Mexicans were very eager to establish statehood and govern themselves. Once again, in 1833, Austin made his way to Mexico City to lobby for separation of the Mexican state of Coahuila and Texas. Austin's proposal did not impress the Mexican government—so, as a reward, they incarcerated him for two years to pay for his crime. When Austin returned to his home in Texas, he took command of the Texas forces of revolting colonists against Mexico—his jailers; however, Austin's command was short-lived, he was replaced by Samuel "Sam" Houston. To further aid the cause, Austin went to Washington to obtain finances and military equipment and supplies for the war effort.

On March 6, 1836, about 6,000 Mexican forces under General Santa Ana marched into San Antonio to quell the Texas rebellion. Making a stand at the Alamo, an old Franciscan mission (first known as Mission San Antonio de Valero) with strong, defensible walls were 186 Texans under Colonels William B. Travis and James "Jim" Bowie. When Gen. Ana demanded their surrender, they responded with artillery fire. The Mexicans raised the red flag, which meant that the Americans would receive no quarter, and after 12 days of cannon-fire the Mexican infantry stormed the battered walls of the Alamo and 186 Texans were dead. Col. Travis with rifle in hand lay next to an artillery piece; Col. Bowie, suffering from pneumonia, lay bayoneted on his cot; while Col. Davy Crockett had been mutilated. Gen. Ana ordered all of their remains to be piled up and burned. A few weeks later, General Sam Houston surprised Mexican forces and captured Gen. Santa Ana on the banks of the San Jacinto River near Galveston Bay and freed Texas.

After Texas had won their independence, Austin ran for the honor of being the first president of the Lone Star Republic of Texas but lost to Houston, who carried about eighty percent of the 6,000 votes cast. In order to continue serving, Stephen Austin became

Houston's secretary of state—he died that same year (1836). To remember him, the city of Austin, Texas was named in his honor. Austin was first settled in 1838 and called Waterloo. It was chosen as the capital of the Republic of Texas in 1839 and renamed Austin. Texas became a state in 1845 and Austin was named the State capital.

Moses' frontier, pioneering life lasted only 60 years, in his "Memorandum" he wrote about the poor, westward-bound "pilgrims" and their trials, tribulations, and hardships they endured along the way. From the Missouri Ozarks to Texas, brave souls looking for freedom and prosperity found much of what they were searching for—but, also struggle and strife. The Lone Star State of Texas remembered the Alamo and never forgot the sacrifices of the heroes that made it all possible—but for Moses Austin, he never lived to see it. His gravestone at Potosi serves as a constant reminder of the many tales that populate the Ozarks.

Bibliography

Athearn, Robert G., *American Heritage New Illustrated History of the United States*, Vol. 6, *The Frontier*, Fawcett Publications, Inc., One Astor Plaza, New York, N.Y., 1963.

Austin, Moses, "A Memorandum of M. Austin's Journey from the Lead Mines in the County of Wythe in the State of Virginia to the Lead Mines in the Province of Louisiana West of the Mississippi, 1796-1797." *American Historical Review*, 1900.

Chronicle of America, Chronicle Publications, Mount Kisco, New York, 1989.

Crain, Mary Beth, *Haunted U.S. Battlefields: Ghosts, Hauntings, and Eerie Events from America's Fields of Honor*, Globe Pequot Press, Guilford, Connecticut, 2008.

Faragher, John Mack; Buhle, Mari Jo; Czitrom, Daniel; Armitage, Susan H., *Out of Many: A History of the American People*, Prentice Hall, Upper Saddle River, New Jersey, 1997.

Funk & Wagnalls New Encyclopedia, Funk & Wagnalls, Inc., New York, 1979.

McCandless, Perry; Foley, William E., *Missouri: Then and Now*, University of Missouri Press, Columbia, Missouri, 1976.

Parrish, William E.; Jones, Jr., Charles T.; Christensen, Lawrence O., *Missouri: The Heart of the Nation*, Forum Press, Inc., Arlington Heights, Illinois, 1980.

Saults, Dan, *Who Was Moses Austin*, The Ozarks Mountaineer, Vol. 29, No. 8 & 9, 1981.

Additional Illustrations

The Jacob Wolf House in Norfork, Arkansas.

Outside staircase of the Jacob Wolf House in Norfork, Arkansas.

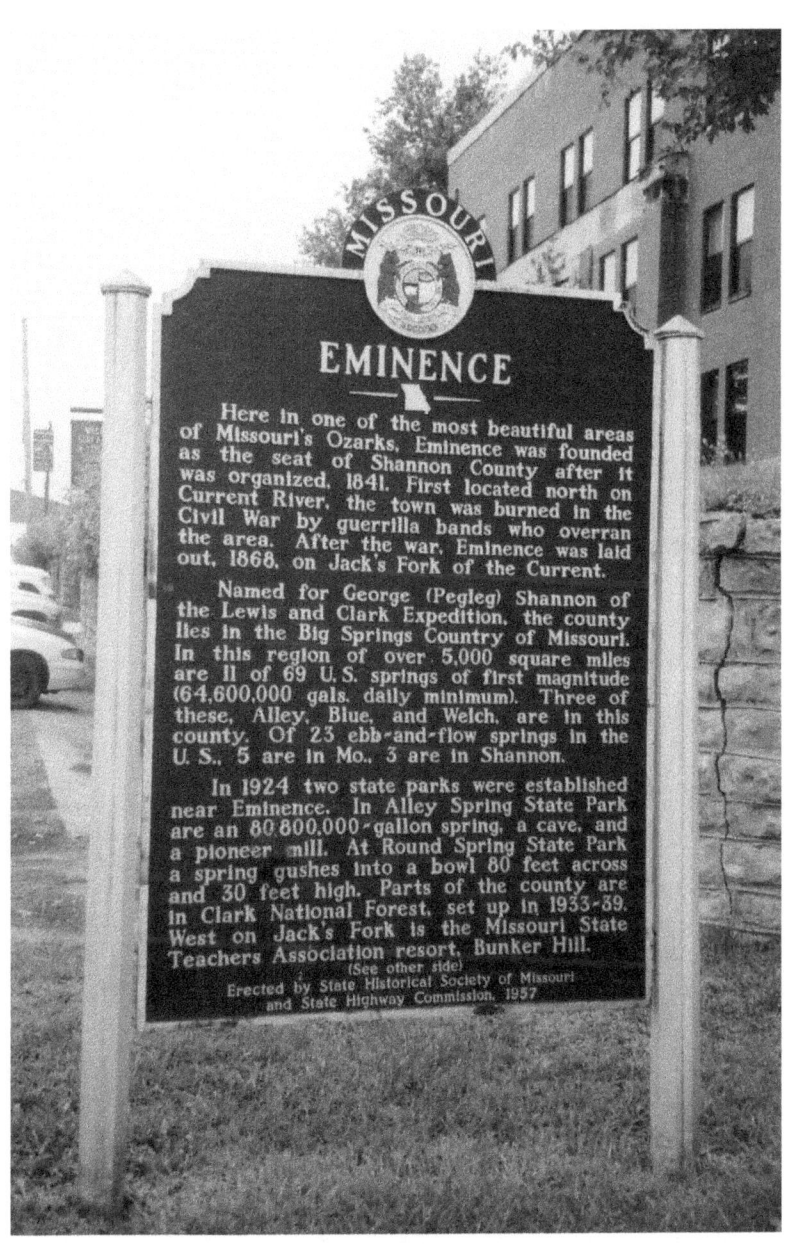

Historic marker in Eminence, Missouri.

Hodgson Mill near Gainesville, Missouri.

Dawt Mill near Gainesville, Missouri.

War Eagle Mill near Rogers, Arkansas.

Historic marker in McDonald County, Missouri.

Downtown Eureka Springs, Arkansas.

Eureka Springs Carnegie Public Library in Eureka Springs, Arkansas.

Ha Ha Tonka Watertower at Ha Ha Tonka State Park near Camdenton, Missouri.

Monument to Mickey Mantle in Commerce, Oklahoma.

APPENDIX

Alf Bolin:
The Death of an Ozarks Outlaw

During the chaos of the American Civil War, thieves and murderers roamed the countryside to take advantage of the situation. Bushwhackers and ruffians that were too lazy to do honest work or were going through "ruff" times and dreamed of the "easy" life, found the lawless era suitable to their liking; it also gave opportunity for some of them to participate in the war the way they wanted to—uncivilized warfare.

About the Ozark terrain in the area, in the *Official Records of the Union and Confederate Armies*, Union Brigadier General Thomas W. Sweeny writing from Springfield, Missouri on July 27, 1861, to Brig. Gen. Nathaniel Lyon, writes about a skirmish that occurred at Forsyth on July 22 that offers a description of the landscape and that turbulent period: "The country through which we passed is exceedingly hilly and broken...." When we approached "the town I took every possible precaution to prevent the hostile force assembled there from becoming aware of our presence." After Gen. Sweeny's advance guard of a company of Kansas Rangers encountered a "picket guard of the enemy some 3 ½ miles from town," two of them were captured. One of the prisoners, remarking about Gen. Sweeny's small force, said that: "If that is all you have, you will get badly whipped, for we have a thousand men in

Forsyth." With a robust cannonade of "shell and canister" and "a well-directed volley," the rebels inhabiting the town were eventually dispersed as they hightailed it to the safety of the wooded Ozarks countryside.

Gen. Sweeny reported that they killed about 8 or 10 and wounded "several times that number." The battle lasted about an hour. The victors gained a sizable amount of goods and equipment stored in the courthouse which was being "used as a barracks for their troops."

The lay-of-the-land in the Ozarks offered a perfect vantage ground for bushwhackers to prosecute their "dirty" work. The hills and hollows, trees and rocks gave excellent cover to these outlaws bent on a life of crime. This sort of dangerous trail may have been what helped to inspire author Harold Bell Wright, when he wrote in his Ozarks book *The Shepherd of the Hills* about the "Old Trail along the higher sunlit ground, followed, also, the other trail down into the valley where the gloomy shadows are...." One such place located a few miles south of Kirbyville, Mo. on Highway JJ not far from the Arkansas border, was too tempting for criminals to ignore—a geological formation of bluffs and boulders that history remembers as the "Murder Rocks" or "Alf Bolin Rocks."

In those days, Alf Bolin's Murder Rocks were along a well-used wagon trail that wound from Little Rock, Ark., to Springfield, Mo.—locals called the trace the "Carrollton-Forsyth Road" or sometimes the "Springfield-Harrison Road." The area became the heinous haunt of Bolin (Bolen) and his gang of lowlifes. Along this remote trail among the giant boulders and rugged Ozark terrain, Bolin and his men ambushed, held up and murdered many unsuspecting souls passing by.

The details surrounding Alf Bolin's short, turbulent life have been the stuff of legends handed down throughout the years by word-of-mouth and by historical research. It is believed that he grew up near the hamlet of Ponce De Leon in present-day Stone County, Mo. He was raised by his grandparents, the Clouds, and became a skillful hunter, trapper and woodsman. When the Civil War broke out, Bolin reportedly rode with Missouri guerrilla Sam Hildebrand in southeast Missouri. Before long, however, he returned to his

Alf Bolin

Ozark homeland and gathered together a small force to continue his campaign against the Union and to terrorize the countryside—threatening all if its remaining citizens. His familiarity with every "nook" and "cranny" of the region made his merciless endeavors unstoppable.

Alf Bolin's reign of terror would eventually come full circle—returning upon *him*! As the tale goes, the federal government had placed a sizable bounty of $5,000 upon his head—dead or alive. The dangerous task of bringing Bolin to justice left some bounty hunters themselves dead at the hands of their black-hearted quarry. Bolin's demise would finally come at the home of Robert Foster, which was not far from the Murder Rocks in an area called the Old Layton Mill.

On February 2, 1863, the infamous bushwhacker would attend a dinner at the Foster log cabin. A Union soldier of the Iowa Volunteer Cavalry, Corporal Zachariah "Zach" Thomas, was also present at the home dressed in civilian clothing and incognito. After dinner, apparently Bolin's last meal, the outlaw leaned into the fireplace to light his pipe, or was possibly warming himself by the cozy fire when Corp. Thomas quickly seized his opportunity and clubbed Bolin repeatedly until he was dead with a fireplace poker.

After the deed was at long last done, the body of Alf Bolin was taken to Forsyth where a man named Colbert Hays reportedly cut off his head with an ax. The headless corpse was buried nearby somewhere along Swan Creek Road while his head was transported to Ozark, Mo., impaled on a long pole by the Union army and displayed for everyone to see for several days. The spectacle was said to be further enhanced by some kids that took the liberty of throwing stones at the poled-head and making keepsakes from its hair and beard.

The $5,000 reward for Alf Bolin was given to Corp. Thomas. As for the abused, severed head, no one knows for certain what became of it. The only thing that is for sure, however, is that Bolin left this world as violently as he had lived in it.

Index

INDEX

A

Abel, Annie Heloise, 75
Alley, John, 83
Anderson, "Bloody Bill", 35, 90, 91
Anderson, Clay, 62
Anderson, Mo., 99
Arkansas *Gazette*, 52
Ashford, Conn., 1
Austin, Moses, 127, 128, 130

B

Batesville, Ark., 64
Baton Rouge, La., 3
Baxter Springs, Kan., 88, 92, 93, 94, 95
Belton, Mo., 15
Bentonville, Ark., 28, 29, 30, 100
Bingham, George Caleb, 92
Birge, John W., 42
Blair, Charles W., 93
Blunt, James G., 75, 94, 95
Boonville, Mo., 55
Breckenridge, Mo., 50
Britton, Wiley, 93, 94

C

Camdenton, Mo., 108, 109
Cane Hill, Ark., 75
Carnegie, Andrew, 113, 114, 115, 116
Carthage, Ill., 51
Carthage, Mo., 55, 69, 97, 99, 100, 112, 113, 115
Carver, George Washington, 61
Cassville, Mo., 6, 85, 86, 101
Cassville *Republican*, 85
Cedar City, Utah, 51
Commerce, Okla., 22, 26
Connelley, William Elsey, 91, 92, 93
Cooperstown, N.Y., 24
Crites, John, 93
Crittenden, Thomas, 36
Crockett, Davy, 64
Curtis, Samuel R., 30

D

Dalton, Bill, Bob, Grat, & Emmett, 77
Daugherty, Roy "Arkansas Tom", 77
Davis, Jefferson, 2
Dimmitt, George H., 119, 120
Doolin, Bill, 77
Dorsey, Caleb, 42

E

Gallatin, Mo., 37, 5

Index

Eminence, Mo., 80, 82
Eureka Springs, Ark., 15, 84
Ewing, Thomas, 90, 91
Exeter, Mo., 85, 86

F

Fitzgerald, David, 62
Ford, Bob, 36
Fort Scott, Kan., 67, 93
Fort Smith, Ark., 72, 73, 74, 75, 76, 77, 78
Fort Smith *Elevator*, 78
Fort Snelling, Minn., 73
Francher, Alexander, 47
Franklin, Benjamin, 119
Frost, Daniel M., 3, 4

G

Gallatin, Mo., 37, 50
Gloyd, Charles, 12
Glover, John M., 42
Goldsby, Crawford, 77
Grant, Ulysses S., 61, 76
Greer, Dabbs, 38
Grove, Okla., 10, 96, 104, 105

H

Halleck, H.W., 43, 90
Hallsville, Mo., 41
Harney, Williams S., 4
Harper's *Weekly*, 51, 52
Harrison, Ark., 46, 47
Haun, Jacob, 50

Hoboken, N.J., 23, 24
Hornet, Mo., 18, 20
Houston, Sam, 64, 84
Howland, James T., 41
Humansville, Mo., 118, 119, 120
Humansville *Star Leader*, 119

I

Izard, George, 63

J

Jackson, Andrew, 84
Jackson, Claiborne Fox, 2, 55, 56
James, Frank, 34, 35, 91
James, Jesse, 32, 33, 34, 35, 36, 37, 38, 39
Jones, Harvey and Bernice, 105, 106, 107
Joplin *Globe*, 98
Joplin, Mo., 25, 100

K

Kansas City *Journal*, 110
Kansas City, Mo., 110, 115
Kearney, Mo., 33, 36
King, Henry, 37

L

Lamar, Mo., 58
Lane, James H., 67, 68, 69, 89

Index

Lawrence, Kan., 35, 91
Lee, John D., 52, 53
Lee, Robert E., 5
Lexington *Kentucky Gazette*, 35
Lexington, Mo., 55
Liberty, Mo., 34, 36, 38, 50
Liberty *Tribune*, 48
Lincoln, Abraham, 2, 8, 61, 67
Lyon, Nathaniel, 1, 2, 3, 4, 5, 6, 7, 8, 56, 57

M

Mantle, Mickey, 24, 25, 26
Maris, Roger, 25
Marmaduke, John S., 56, 57
Maury, Dabnery H., 4
McCaskill, George Washington, 83
McCorkle, John, 89, 92, 94
McCulloch, Ben, 6, 7, 8, 30
McKinley, William, 13
Monegaw Springs, Mo., 85
Moore, Carrie, 12
Mt. Vernon, Mo., 123

N

Nation, Carry, 12, 13, 14, 15
Nation, David A., 12
Neosho, Mo., 39, 100
Nevada, Mo., 67
New Madrid, Mo., 20
New York City, N.Y., 23
New York *Sun*, 53
Noel, Mo., 98, 99

Norfork, Ark., 60, 62
Nuttall, Thomas, 73

O

Osceola, Mo., 66, 68, 69, 70

P

Palmyra, Mo., 41
Parker, Isaac C., 76, 77, 78
Pea Ridge, Ark., 30, 31, 75
Phelps, Mary W., 8
Pineville *Democrat*, 37, 38
Pineville, Mo., 33, 37, 39, 100
Pond, James B., 93, 94
Prairie Grove, Ark., 35, 37, 75
Prentiss, Benjamin M., 41, 42, 43
Price, Sterling, 3, 5, 6, 7, 30, 55, 69, 70

Q

Quantrill, William Clarke, 34, 35, 89, 90, 91, 92, 93, 94, 95
Quapaw, Okla., 20

R

Robinson, Jackie, 24
Rogers, Ark., 99
Ruth, Babe, 25

Index

S

Shelby, Joseph O., 35, 36, 37, 70
Sigel, Franz, 6, 29, 30, 31
Smith, Joseph, 48, 49, 51
Snead, Thomas L., 5, 55
Snyder, R.M., 109, 110
Southwest City, Mo., 39
Spavinaw, Okla., 24
Springfield, Mo., 58, 105, 124
Stamping Ground, Kentucky, 34
Starr, Belle, 77
Starr, Henry, 77, 78
St. Joseph, Mo., 35
St. Louis, Mo., 1, 2, 3, 55, 67, 75
St. Louis *Republican*, 35, 76
Stuart, "Jeb", 8
Sweeney, T.W., 6

T

Thorp, Joseph, 48
Tipton, Mo., 75

V

Van Dorn, Earl, 30, 31
Verona, Mo., 124

W

Wagner, Honus, 24
War Eagle, Ark., 106
Waverly, Mo., 35

Webb, W.L., 31, 92
Wichita, Kan., 13
Wolf, Jacob, 62, 63, 64

Y

Young, Brigham, 48, 51
Young, Cy, 24
Younger, Cole, 36, 91
Younger, Jim, 36, 91
Younger, John, 85

Other Books by Rex T. Jackson

The Sultana Saga: The Titanic of the Mississippi
James B. Eads: The Civil War Ironclads and His Mississippi
A Trail of Tears: The American Indian in the Civil War
Traces of Ozarks Past: Outlaws, Icons, and Memorable Events
Notable Persons and Places in Missouri's History

About the Author

Rex T. Jackson's work has appeared in a number of publications, like *The Ozarks Mountaineer, Blue and Gray, Good Old Days, Ancient American, Capper's Weekly, Back Home, The Ozarks Reader, Route 66 Magazine* and others. He became a staff member of *The Ozarks Mountaineer* (based in the Branson, Missouri area) for several years and eventually founded *The Ozarks Reader Regional Magazine* and served as publisher and editor from 2004 through 2012.

www.ingramcontent.com/pod-product-compliance
Lightning Source LLC
Chambersburg PA
CBHW050637160426
43194CB00010B/1705